A BAND DIRECTOR'S GUIDE TO BEGINNING WOODWINDS

John M. Denis, Ph.D.

Cover and Interior Design
FARHAN SHAHID

Published by Agogic Press
A division of Denis Media LLC
780 W FM 1626 #174, Manchaca, TX 78652

Copyright © 2026 by Agogic Press

All rights reserved. No part of this book may be reproduced, transmitted, stored, distributed, or used in any printed or electronic form without written permission from the publisher.

Printed in the United States of America
First Edition: 2026
ISBN: 978-1-7332967-5-5

Every effort has been made to obtain appropriate permission for materials included in this book; any oversights will be corrected, once communicated, in future editions.

ACKNOWLEDGEMENTS

To Misty Smith, Lori Bryson, Lisa Fitts, Katie Lewis, Kristin Hames, Dr. Vanguel Tangarov, Dr. Adah Jones, Dr. Todd Oxford, Daris W Hale, Rob Chilton, and everyone else who has helped me expand my own horizons in the world of woodwinds.

CONTENTS

Introduction 13
    How to Use this Book 14
    Planning Matters 14
    Familiarity Breeds Expertise 15
    Prioritization and Flexibility 15
    Commonalities 16
    Assessment 18
    Notation 19
    Resources 19

Flute 21
    Instrument Selection 22
    Equipment 23
    Assembly 24
    Tone Production and Embouchure 26
    Embouchure Lesson Plan/Instruction Sequence 27
    Register Changes 29
    Articulation 29
    Articulation Lesson Plan/Instruction Sequence 30
    Playing Position 32
    Intonation 35
    Vibrato 36
    Ideal Aural Images 36
    Selected Resources 36
    Beginner Flute Sequence Example 37
    Practical Tips 38
    Troubleshooting Flute 44
    Flute Fingerings 46
    Flute Supplemental Exercises 48

Double Reeds 54

Oboe 57
- Instrument Selection 59
- Equipment 59
- Assembly 60
- Tone Production and Embouchure 61
- Embouchure Lesson Plan/Instructional Sequence 62
- Articulation 63
- Articulation Lesson Plan 64
- Playing Position 65
- Intonation 66
- Dynamics 67
- Vibrato 67
- Special Techniques 68
- Ideal Aural Images 69
- Selected Beginner Repertoire 69
- Beginner Oboe Sequence Example 69
- Practical Tips 70
- Troubleshooting Oboe 74
- Oboe Fingerings 77
- Oboe supplemental exercises 79

Bassoon 85
- Instrument Selection 86
- Equipment 87
- Assembly 88
- Tone Production and Embouchure 88
- Embouchure Lesson Plan/Instructional Sequence 90
- Articulation 91
- Articulation Lesson Plan 91
- Playing Position 92

Intonation 94
Vibrato 95
Special Techniques 96
Ideal Aural Images 96
Selected Beginner Repertoire 97
Beginner Bassoon Sequence Example 97
Practical Tips 98
Troubleshooting Bassoon 100
Beginner Bassoon Fingerings 103
Bassoon Supplemental Exercises 105

Single Reeds 113
Mouthpiece and Ligature 115

Clarinet 119
Instrument Selection 121
Equipment 122
Assembly 123
Tone Production and Embouchure 124
Embouchure Lesson Plan/Instructional Sequence 127
Articulation 128
Articulation Lesson Plan and Instructional Sequence 129
Playing Position 130
Intonation 131
Technical Considerations 132
The Clarinet Family 135
Ideal Aural Images 136
Selected Resources 137
Practical Tips 137
Beginner Clarinet Sequence Example 142

Troubleshooting Clarinet 144
Clarinet Fingerings 147
Clarinet Supplemental Exercises 150

Saxophone 157

Instrument Selection 159
Equipment 160
Assembly 161
Tone Production and Embouchure 162
Embouchure Lesson Plan/Instructional Sequence 164
Articulation 165
Articulation Lesson Plan/Instructional Sequence 166
Playing Position 168
Intonation 169
Vibrato 171
The Saxophone Family 171
Ideal Aural Images 172
Selected Beginner Resources 173
Practical Tips 173
Troubleshooting Saxophone 178
Saxophone Fingerings 181
Sax Supplemental Exercises 183

References 188

Heterogeneous Exercises 190

About the Author 227

LIST OF FIGURES

Figure I-1 Finger Numbers 17

Figure F-3 Teardrop/Cupid's Bow 22

Figure F-1 Flute Ranges 22

Figure F-2 Flute Skill Ranges 22

Figure F-4 Parts of the Flute 24

Figure F-5 Flute Assembly 25

Figure F-6 Flute Embouchure 27

Figure F-7 Flute Hand Position 33

Figure F-8 Flute Playing Position 33

Figure F-9 Flute Tuning Notes 35

Figure F-10 Flute Intonation Challenges 35

Figures D-1 and D-2 Oboe and Bassoon Reeds 55

Figure O-1 Oboe Range 58

Figure O-2 Oboe Skill Range 58

Figure O-3 English Horn Range 58

Figure O-4 Oboe Parts 59

Figure O-5 Oboe Assembly 60

Figure O-6 Oboe Embouchure 62

Figure O-7 Oboe Playing Position 65

Figure O-8 Oboe Tuning Notes 66

Figure O-9 Oboe Intonation Challenges 66

Figure O-10 Oboe F Fingerings 68

Figure B-1 Bassoon Ranges 86

Figure B-2 Bassoon Skill Ranges 86

Figure B-3 Bassoon Parts 87

Figure B-4 Bassoon Assembly 88

Figure B-5 Bassoon Embouchure Figure B-5 Bassoon Embouchure 89

Figure B-7 Bassoon Hand Position 93

Figure B-6 Bassoon Playing Position 93

Figure B-8 Bassoon Tuning Notes 94

Figure B-9 Bassoon Intonation Challenges 95

Figure SR-1 Reed Diagram 114

Figure SR-2 Mouthpieces 116

Figure SR-3 Reed Seal/Touch Point 117

Figure C-1 Clarinet Range 120

Figure C-2 Clarinet Skill Ranges 120

Figure C-3 Bass Clarinet Range 120

Figure C-4 Clarinet Parts 122

Figure C-5 Clarinet Assembly 123

Figure C-6 Clarinet Embouchure 126

Figure C-7 Clarinet Playing Position 130

Figure C-8 Clarinet Hand Position 131

Figure C-9 Clarinet Tuning Notes 131

Figure C-10 Clarinet Intonation Challenges 132

Figure C-11 Clarinet Registers 133

Figure C-12 Resonance Fingerings 134

Figure S-1 Alto Range 158

Figure S-2 Bari Range 158

Figure S-3 Soprano Range 158

Figure S-4 Tenor Range 159

Figure S-5 Sax Skill Ranges 159

Figure S-6 Sax Parts 160

Figure S-7 Sax Assembly 162

Figure S-8 Saxophone Embouchure 164

Figure S-9 Saxophone Playing Position 168

Figure S-10 Saxophone Hand Position 169

Figure S-11 Saxophone Tuning Notes 170

Figure S-12 Saxophone Intonation Concerns 170

INTRODUCTION

HOW TO USE THIS BOOK

If you're reading this, then you have at least a passing interest in learning how to teach beginning woodwind instruments. Fantastic. What you will find in the following pages are thoughts, approaches, and teaching strategies informed by the experiences of many skilled music educators, not just myself. I've attempted to synthesize the material and draw out the fundamental information and approaches that will help novice teachers to build a strong foundation in beginning woodwind instruction. More experienced band directors may also find the knowledge contained therein a great refresher (with perhaps a few new tools to add to the toolbox).

This book is meant to lay a solid foundation for band directors/public school educators in working with beginning woodwinds. It is a solid starting point from which to build; none of the material is absolute or exhaustive. Use this book as a resource rather than a rulebook and build upon the information and exercises to create your own beginning woodwind curriculum. Each instrument section will include example lessons for embouchure and articulation and are formatted so that readers can use the book as a guidebook, flipping to the desired instrument and accessing the information quickly.

PLANNING MATTERS

Planning is one of the legs of what I have referred to elsewhere as the "effective teaching triad"[1], which consists of planning, assessment, and reflection (more on those later). Learning how to play an instrument is a complex and challenging task that requires significant time and effort investment from students and their families. Providing students with an optimal environment and instruction to help them succeed is an important responsibility held by band directors, and planning is an essential component of quality instruction.

So many teachers fall back on past experiences or intuition instead of careful planning.[2] For example, scholars have found that immediate and intentional repetition is one of the least effective ways to memorize something[3], yet band directors often fall into the habit of repetition with no context or intentionality to build memorization. Correct repetitions in the moment, asking for correct performance after a period of working on something else, guiding student focus toward the reason for the reps, and other types of encoding and recall practice are more effective in more situations than just repeating with no context. However, this takes planning. It is much harder to consistently deliver the right kinds of repetition on the fly than it is to just fake it 'til you make it.

And make no mistake, faking it is a much slower process at the beginning of an instrumental journey. Time spent trying to identify issues is often inconsistent, inefficient, and ineffective without the necessary musical knowledge and lesson planning. Think of it like trying to spot one out of place puzzle piece without knowing what the image is supposed to look like when you start; the task becomes harder, slower, and less consistent without the reference image.

---

1   Denis, *Program Notes: A Comprehensive Guide to Band Directing,* 2022, p39, 49.
2   Learning Express, 2009, 98.
3   Brown, Roediger, and McDaniel, *Make it Stick: The Science of Successful Learning,* 2014, p46.

Introduction

FAMILIARITY BREEDS EXPERTISE

Yes, I know that this common phrase, "Familiarity breeds..." usually leads "contempt" not "expertise." But in the case of something skill based like playing an instrument, familiarity is a crucial part of being an effective teacher, and effective teachers go out of their way to familiarize themselves with the instruments they teach. Let me be perfectly clear here: by "familiarize" I mean learn to play these instruments themselves.

Some may read the previous sentence and balk. I assure you, I do not mean directors must become accomplished professionals on every instrument taught in the classroom. Instead, I mean that the teacher should strive for the ability to make a characteristic sound on every instrument taught at the beginning level and have some basic facility on a technical level. If tone is preeminent (it is), then teachers need to have the skills to facilitate student development of tone. The primary way we as teachers develop this starts with learning how to make a characteristic tone for ourselves on the instruments.

There are caveats, of course. With instruction, most people can make a sound on most instruments, but there are certain physical characteristics that may make it difficult to achieve a successful performance on certain instruments. Tear-drop lip shapes for flute players are perhaps the most well-known example. Individuals with a tear drop on their upper lip can absolutely learn to play flute, but the embouchure differs from those with no tear drop significantly enough that it may add challenge to learning the flute in a class setting. Teachers with teardrops may experience the same challenges as students, and spending time working to overcome the difficulties will better prepare them to help students with the same issue.

Even if you have problems learning how to produce a characteristic tone on an instrument, the time spent working towards that goal will improve your instruction. Invest in learning the instruments.

PRIORITIZATION AND FLEXIBILITY

Not every aspect of instrumental performance can be taught at once, and setting priorities is an important part of sequencing instruction. A sequence is "a logically ordered progression of tiny steps, activities, lessons, or content that lead students towards learning goals and/or objectives"[4] and is a crucial part of any effective teaching, especially at the foundational stages of an activity. In each instrument chapter in this book, I will present a few smaller sequences as well as one larger sequence for teaching the instrument.

These sequences I provide here are based on my own teaching experience of starting students on instruments in groups and the experiences of successful colleagues. From year to year, I tweak sequencing to match my students and their contexts, and I strongly encourage readers to do the same in their own teaching. Think of these sequences as starting templates instead of prescriptive, recipe-like instructions. Always be willing to be flexible and adapt them to suit specific individuals or groups.

---

4   Denis, 2022, p. 42.

COMMONALITIES

While the woodwinds each have many unique qualities, techniques, and requirements for successful performance, there are certain commonalities that will help directors to make connections in heterogeneous classes as well as to build their own understanding. I've included several of my most important commonalities below.

- Assemble woodwinds from the bottom up (towards the mouth) and disassemble them from the top down. Doing so protects the reed (on reed instruments) and the head joint (on flutes). A damaged head joint will lead to tone production problems.

- Avoid torque on keywork when possible. Students should not twist the rods or springs/spring bars as they are easily pushed out of alignment in ways that will affect tone and intonation.

- Keys should be easy to press down and should spring back to their open or closed positions rapidly and with little to no hesitation or obstruction. This is known as key action.

- Pads need to seal properly and must be cared for and replaced to guarantee they are serving their intended purpose. The best way to check if a pad is leaking is to have a leak light and place it inside the instrument, close the pad, and turn off the lights. If you can see any light, then air can also escape. Some woodwinds or keys will have adjustment screws while others will not. Avoid trying to adjust pad height/sealing yourself, unless you are familiar with repair of the instrument and have a way to verify that the pad is sealing.
  - Pad height can affect tone and intonation. Do not adjust pad height unless you are familiar with the particular needs of the instrument.

- Spring bars hold the keys in their proper position (closed or open) and often pop out of place. Get a spring hook to quickly put them back in place. The more often you try to force it with other tools (like a pencil), the more likely it is that eventually a spring bar will get bent or broken.

- Swabbing is done to remove water from the instrument/pads and should take place after every playing session. Do not store wet swabs or cloths inside the instrument, as it prevents full drying and will speed up the degradation of the pads. Use silk/soft cloth swabs whenever possible to avoid the cloth getting stuck in the instrument (I prefer silk).

- No woodwinds like water/moisture. Reeds can easily warp if oversoaked, and they also can behave unpredictably with sudden or dramatic temperature and humidity changes. Wood instruments (oboe, bassoon, clarinet) have the same problem. Once the wood is cracked, it is difficult and expensive to restore the instrument to even a semblance of proper condition. Water is bad for pads and corks as well.

- Breathing to play is different than breathing to live. Students must learn how to properly inhale (using both diaphragm and intercostal muscles) and learn how to sustain exhalation through their instrument. Different woodwinds provide different wind resistance (flute and oboe are essentially polar opposites in this regard), but none of the woodwinds can be played with characteristic tones without a proper inhalation.

Introduction

- ♪ Articulations require proper wind/air support.

- ♪ Eddie Green had a rule that applies to all instruments: "When you play a musical instrument, no part of the body touches any other part of the body."[5] This is a fantastic rule of thumb for instrumental playing position and applies to all of the hand/finger/arm/etc. positions on the woodwinds.

- ♪ Left hands are always closer to the player's face.

- ♪ I prefer to number fingers starting with the closest to the sound production (left index finger = Finger 1) and working my way down to the bottom of the instrument (right ring finger = Finger 6). This allows for continuity between the woodwind instruments as they all share similar finger positions while avoiding confusion among students as to which hand I'm discussing.

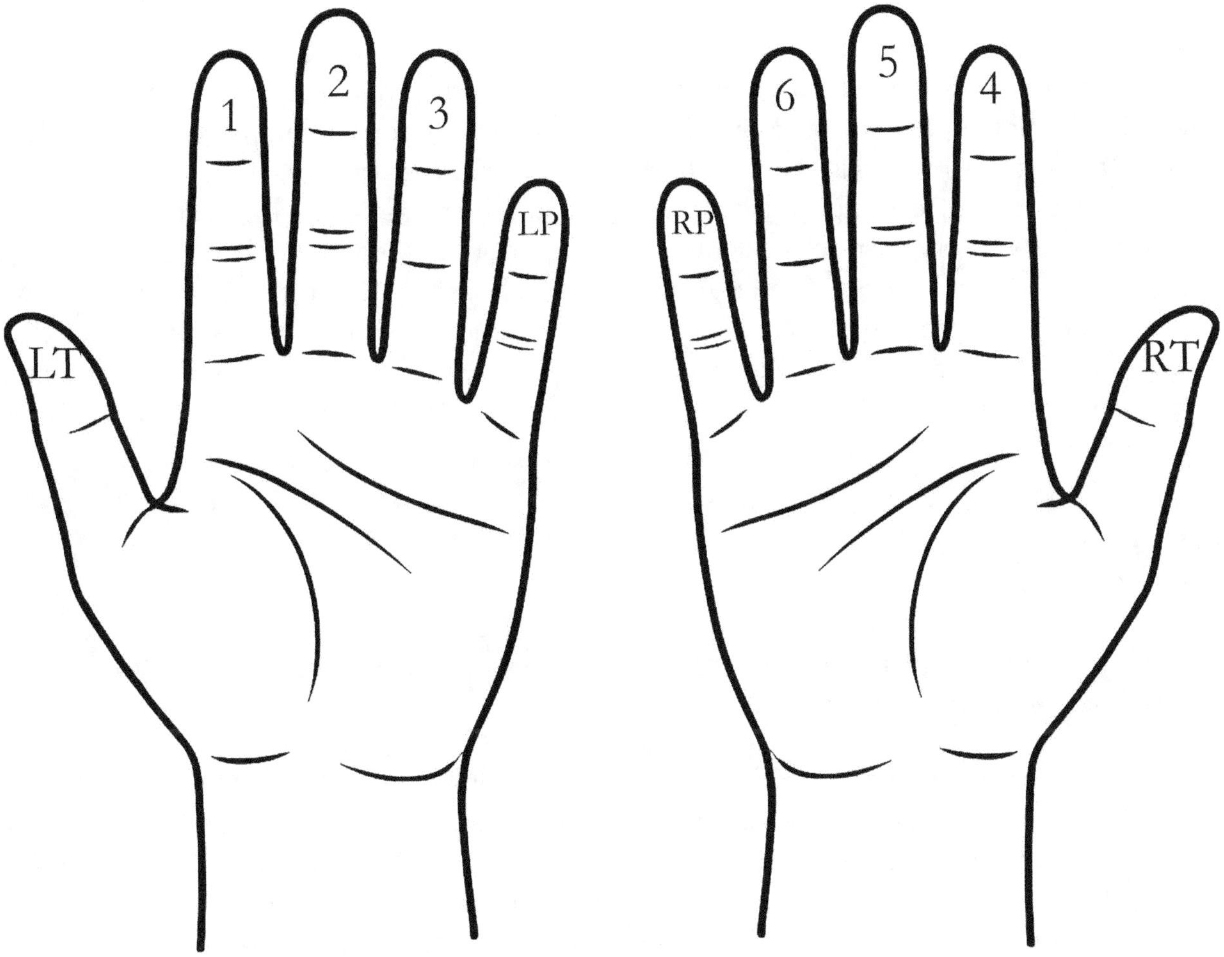

Figure I-1 Finger Numbers

---

5   Cavitt, *On Teaching Band: Notes from Eddie Green*, p. 56. Dr. Cavit is an excellent educator, and Eddie Green was a famous pedagogue – tons of useful information in this book.

- ♪ No woodwind embouchure relies solely on vertical energy (i.e., energy from the teeth/jaw through the center of the lips).

- ♪ There are some commonalities in embouchure across all the instruments, such as "corners come in and/or down instead of back and/or up." Additionally, some of the instrument embouchures have more similarities, like clarinet and oboe corner energy or sax and bassoon squishy but controlled bottom lip, etc., but take care not to draw too many embouchure shape connections between instruments.

- ♪ Griswold[6] wrote that the distance between the wind, through the embouchure, and the vibration source is one of the core aspects of woodwind characteristic tone production. According to Griswold, this refers to the distance between the edge of the bottom lip and flute tone hole, the amount of double reeds placed in the mouth, and the amount of single reed mouthpiece in mouth/top teeth position.

- ♪ Woodwind technique is both simple and challenging. Simple, because the majority of technique can be distilled into two things: holding the instrument properly with little to no tension and continuous repetition of finger patterns. Teachers need to pay close attention to hand/finger position during the early stages of learning the instrument to avoid bad habits or tension, as the best, and perhaps only, way to develop solid technique is through correct repetition of effective finger/scale patterns. It is up to teachers to explicitly instruct students on the importance of repetition for building technique and then lead students through effective repetition in the classroom. This repetition helps develop the muscle memory necessary to cleanly execute a wide variety of common diatonic and scale patterns in all keys and provides opportunity to focus on specific fingering issues unique to each instrument. Teachers should continually reinforce the importance of repetition and at-home practice for building technique.

ASSESSMENT

How do you know that students are successful? How do they know they're successful? What drives your instructional choices? What drives their practice?

In many programs, assessment is the answer to these questions, even if the parties involved have never given it much thought. What you assess in the classroom or lesson setting is what the students view as important, and therefore what they practice (if they practice at all). Furthermore, Duke suggests that instruction is driven by assessment, either intentionally or through happenstance.[7] As part of the planning process, decide on the things that matter for learning each instrument (the fundamentals) and develop assessments to both ascertain if students are successful as well as to communicate importance and success to the students themselves.

---

6   Gene Giswold, *Teaching Woodwinds*, 2008, p. 17.
7   Bob Duke, longtime professor at the University of Texas at Austin, *Intelligent Music Teaching*, 2009, p. 49–87.

NOTATION

While teaching beginners to read is worthy of a full book in itself, keeping in mind two important points around literacy (rhythm and pitch reading) will lay a strong foundation. First is rhythm. Rhythm reading should be taught systematically and consistently. Every teacher needs an effective counting system that they use all the time and that ideally transfers from year to year. The choice of systems is up to you; what matters most is **consistency of use.** Start with covering pulse and work your way into your counting system of choice. *Teaching Rhythm Logically* by Williams provides a definitive guide to systematic rhythm reading. Second is pitch. When it comes to teaching pitch reading, be sure to connect the sound with the symbol instead of just the button. For many young woodwind students, it is easy to equate notes with something like typing; press the correct button and the sound will have to be correct as well. In approaching it that way, they leave some of the aural skills behind that will make far more successful musicians in the long run. I am a huge fan of singing note names (often referred to as "singering") and eventually having them finger along. Pitch reading is about the sound, its symbol, and all the mechanical things that make the correct sound happen. Be sure that your beginners have many opportunities to sight-read as part of the curriculum and structure these activities so that students practice reading skills.

RESOURCES

If my grass needs mowing, the best tool for the job is a lawn mower. If, in a fit of insanity, I pull out a flamethrower instead, it will certainly lessen the amount of grass that I have but it may also burn down my house. Likewise, resources like method books/handouts/curricula/etc. are tools, and like any tools they must be selected by their applicability to the task at hand and the desired outcome. Method books are designed to try and cover the widest topics in average settings and therefore will seldom match an individual program perfectly. What you will read later in this book are approaches to teaching woodwinds based on my experiences, the experiences of other teachers, and the literature on the subject. These aren't the definitive ways to teach beginning woodwinds so much as they are *<u>a way</u>* of teaching woodwinds; one that has worked for students and teachers in the past.

You are I are different people, and your students are different than my students in some ways and like them in many others. Think about the specific methodologies in the rest of the book as a tested approach to build from in order to create lessons and educational experiences that lead to student success. As I often tell my students, the best way of teaching something is the way that helps the student demonstrate learning—that's it. **If it leads a student to success, then it's a successful method.**

For a more in-depth discussion of running a beginning band program, see chapter 6, "Beginning Band" in *Program Notes: A Comprehensive Guide to Band Directing* (GIA, 2023). I have also included a list of excellent reference books regarding woodwinds at the end of this text.

I want to finish this introductory section with this thought: Avoid *methodolatry (worshiping one way of teaching)*. Learn from everyone you can, try different approaches (including those in this book), stick with what generates success for your students, and don't be beholden to one method or book for every instrument all the time.

Flute

Due to its simple method of sound production, the flute is one of the oldest instruments in the world. The origins of the modern flute can be traced to 1847 when Theobald Boehm completed his development of the current fingering system. Flute is a C instrument (non-transposing), and notation for flute is written in the sounding range (Figure F-1).

Figure F-1 Flute Ranges

While not rigid, below are approximate beginner, intermediate, and advanced ranges (Figure F-2).

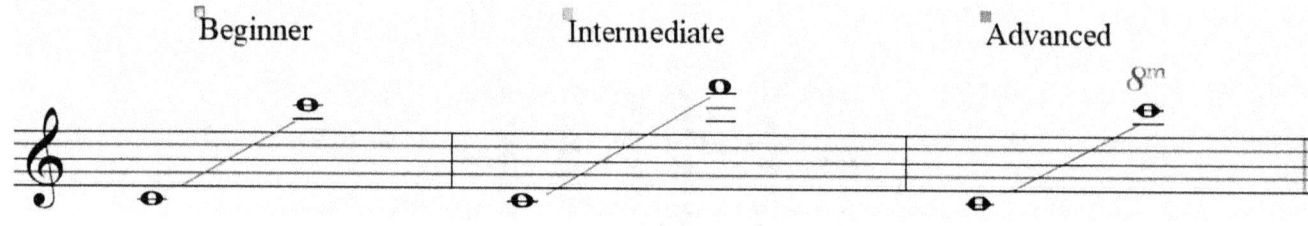

Figure F-2 Flute Skill Ranges

INSTRUMENT SELECTION

When considering flute as a choice for individual students, carefully look at their lips. Top lips with teardrops/Cupid's bow can make initial sound production and higher ranged pitches more difficult (Figure F-3). While not a deal-breaker, I would be upfront with any students who have a teardrop/Cupid's bow as to some of the challenges that lip shape will likely cause in the earlier stages of learning the flute. Additionally, a severe underbite may also lead to difficulty in producing a quality sound, and students with retainer plates may struggle with tone production and articulation; evenly placed teeth lead to greater ease in tone production on flute. There are debates about lip thickness and its relationship to tone production. The most important

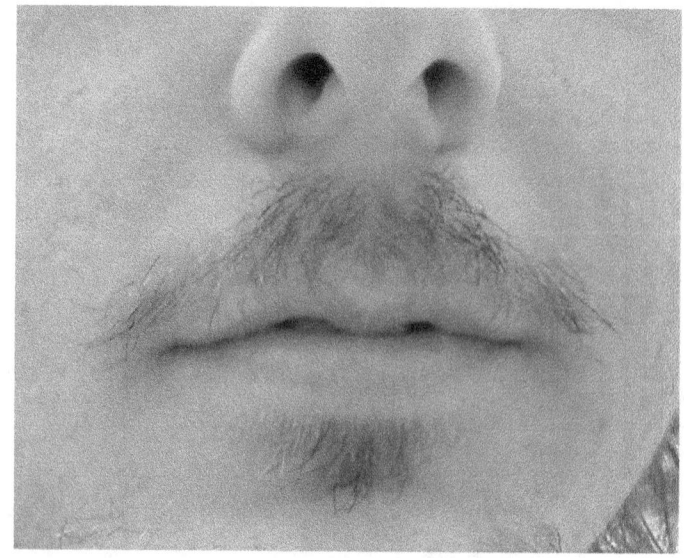

Figure F-3 Teardrop/Cupid's Bow

22

considerations regarding lips are the presence of a tear drop/Cupid's bow and the student's ability to make a pouty bottom lip. Another possible consideration is students with more skin between the bottom of the nose and top of the lip may find flexibility in embouchure easier.

Furthermore, arm and finger length are also important considerations. Some instrument manufacturers have models with curved head joints for students with shorter arms; however, these may be difficult to find or cost more. Additionally, finger dexterity and hand-eye coordination may impact student success and may be taken into account when selecting students for flute. I often test finger dexterity by asking students to tap each of their fingers to their thumb one at a time as quickly as they can in order (left index finger/Finger 1 to pinky). Finally, as flute notation often stretches into ledger lines, students with quality music reading skills often excel further into the band program. This can, and should, be taught and therefore should not be a significant factor in selection; instead, it is another area to inform the wider choice.

EQUIPMENT

In some band director positions, you will have the ability to influence the specific equipment your students procure for band class, which can be daunting on your secondary instruments. Assorted instrument manufacturers have instruments designed for beginning students. I generally prefer open-hole flutes with plugs, as they allow for better tone quality into the student's second or third year while still remaining appropriate for beginners. They also help students to refine hand position by requiring fingers to cover the holes correctly. Students should remove the plugs as soon as their finger pads can seal the holes, and generally should remove them starting with Finger 4, 5, 2, and then 3/6—in that order. I would much rather a student look for a step-up instrument when they have had significant exposure to band and know they are interested in the activity than during or immediately after their beginner year. That being said, closed-hole instruments are suitable for beginners.

Students who have trouble reaching the G key (Finger 3 is on the short side) may want to look into a flute with an offset G key, which extends the G key to a more comfortable position for short fingers. Likewise, students with shorter arms (particularly the right arm) can opt for a curved head joint. I have used such head joints with my smallest students in the past to great results. Ultimately, the instrument should comfortably come to the student in all aspects—embouchure, fingers, etc.

Below are some suggestions for future reference, chosen at the time of publication. (Note that these may change due to model updates and manufacturer quality.) Additionally, do not hesitate to ask other band directors or private instructors for their recommendations.

Flute

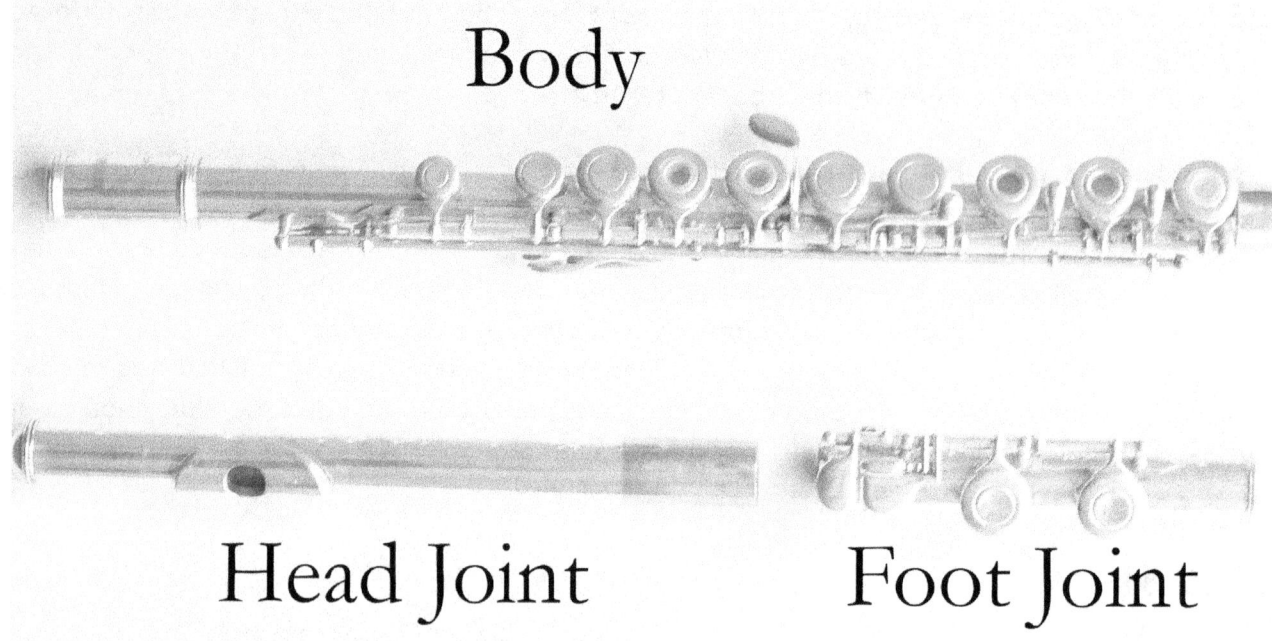

Figure F-4 Parts of the Flute

Instrument	Swab	Mirror
Jupiter 511-RSO or Yamaha YFL-262/282 or Emerson EF6	Silk swab/cloth for Flute	Small enough to easily fit on a music stand

ASSEMBLY

Once you have helped students identify the top of the case, have students place the case flat on the floor before opening. Teach students to recognize and name the parts of the instrument (Figure F-4), as this will save time and confusion later. First, remove the protective cap, if applicable, from the body of the instrument. Then, begin with the foot joint and body, having students carefully hold both parts where there are no keys or rods. One the foot joint this will mean gripping it from the back (palm against the instrument, not the rod) while the body should predominantly be handled by the tenon near the top where there is no keywork (most manufacturers put their logo here). The bottom of the body has exposed metal at the joint and typically does not have the instrument brand or model. Next, gently slide the body into the foot joint with a slight twisting motion/rotation until the foot joint is flush with the body and the foot joint rod is centered with the keys (specifically the key for finger 6).

Finally, remove the head joint cap, if applicable, and slide the head joint into the open end of the body, being careful to hold the body without touching rods or keys and avoid gripping the lip plate/embouchure hole. The embouchure hole should align with the center of the keys on the body and the head joint should never be pushed in all the way. Strive for a little less than a quarter of an inch (or three quarters stacked together)

as a starting point. Some models of beginner flute have arrows on the various parts to facilitate placement; however, students should know the correct placement based on hole-key alignment for future reference or in case such markings are absent. Teachers can mark both the head joint and body with a dot of nail polish to help them place the head joint consistently.

Assembly concerns often repeat from year-to-year and student-to-student. Constantly assess head joint/foot joint alignment until students have successfully demonstrated mastery. If either the foot or the head joint is difficult to slide onto the body, clean the exposed metal, as sticking is most often caused by excess material/gunk (technical term) in the tenons. In an absolute emergency, pencil lead might help lubricate the joints for assembly. If using this approach, students or teachers **must clean the tenons** once disassembled. To clean the tenon on a daily basis, simply wipe both the tenon and the receiver with a clean, microfiber cloth. For a deeper clean, rub paraffin wax on either the tenon or the receiver (not both) and assemble the two pieces normally with a slight twisting motion. Then, disassemble the parts, once again with a slight rotation. The exposed tenon will likely have a black or specked film; wipe both the exposed tenon and the receiver with a clean cloth. Damp cloths can also be used, but take great care not to get the pads or corks wet.

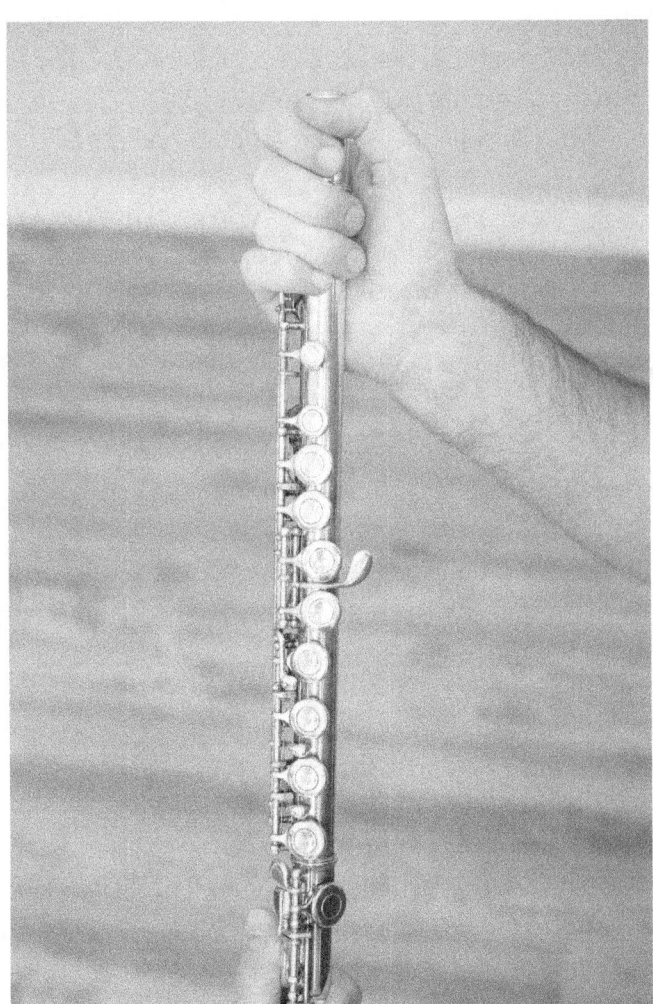
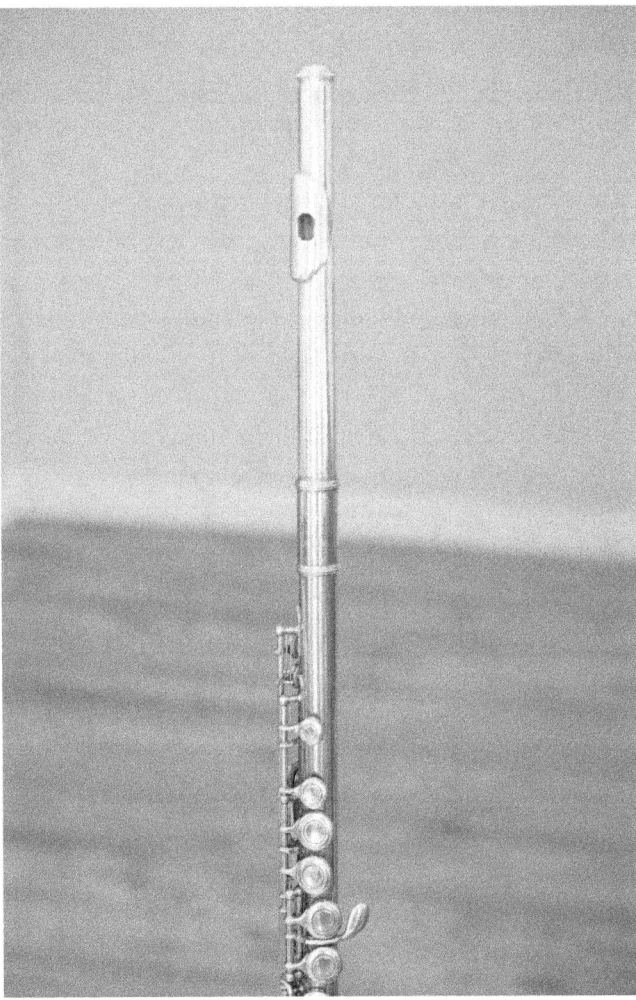

Figure F-5 Flute Assembly

TONE PRODUCTION AND EMBOUCHURE

All sound is caused by vibration, and on flute the wind column splits as it strikes the far edge of the embouchure hole, producing a vibrating column of air known as an *edge tone*. The nature of the edge tone requires accuracy of wind stream placement, wind direction, and wind focus, which is made more complicated by the lack of tactile internal sensations during performance. For these reasons, head joint placement is of paramount importance for flutists. Directors should take great care to develop accuracy of head joint placement by helping students find the "sweet spot" where the embouchure hole is correctly aligned with their lips.

As shown in Figure F-6, the embouchure hole should be mostly centered on the face with the head joint parallel to the lips/embouchure hole parallel to the aperture. For students with teardrops or uneven top lips, their sweet spot will be off center. Similarly, vertical placement of the head joint can affect tone quality. The bottom lip should cover a portion of the embouchure hole; however, the amount varies based on lip shape and performance range. Generally speaking, students with thin lips will need to cover more of the embouchure hole (approximately ⅓) and students with thick lips will need to cover less (approximately ¼). Covering too much of the embouchure hole will create a small/thin tone, restrict dynamic range, sound flat, and impede clear articulation. In contrast, covering too little will require even greater wind use, spread the tone, limit performance range (particularly in the third octave), sound sharp, and restrict dynamics.

Teachers can check for correct centering of the sweet spot by observing the condensation trail that forms on the lip plate as students blow across the embouchure hole. The ideal condensation trail is conical (triangle-shaped) and centered across the embouchure hole. Take the time to help students find the perfect sweet spot, where the condensation is aligned accurately and the vertical placement is correct. Then have them practice placing the head joint in their sweet spot multiple times using their mirrors.

The flute embouchure should be relaxed and flexible, with students' lips moving slightly forward to the lip plate in a pout movement. One way to introduce this concept to students is to have them say the syllable "pooh," which will mimic the lip motion and shape. Saying the "pooh" syllable causes the lips to move slightly forward, and the corners move towards the canine teeth, creating an oval or round aperture as the wind flows through the lips. Flutists must avoid smiling, creating an extremely flat aperture while blowing, or bringing their bottom lip over the teeth. Finally, be certain that students are keeping their jaw/teeth even and that they are not excessively pressing the lip plate into their faces.

When making their first sounds, students may feel like the flute requires a significantly greater volume of wind than expected (or than other instruments). This is largely due to the lack of backpressure, wind control, and the efficiency (or lack thereof) of the edge tone. Avoid working on sustained long tones early in the process, as students will make embouchure adjustments to regulate their wind instead of starting with proper inhalation. Instead, continue to work natural inhalation/exhalation and be patient, as support and control will come to flutists as their embouchure develops.

Flute

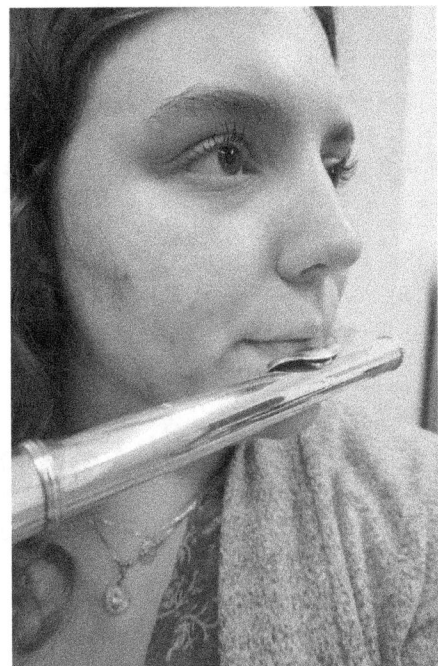
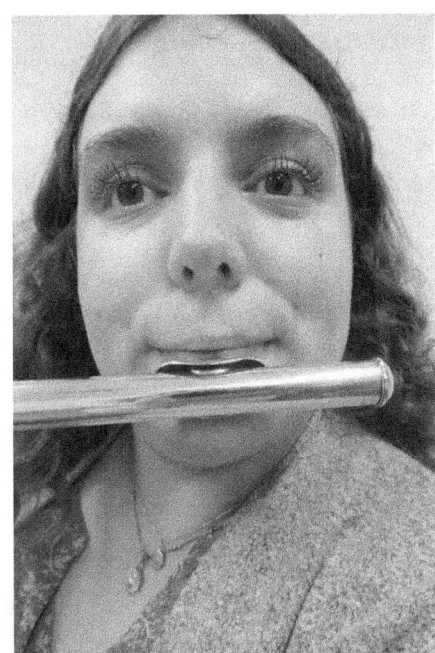

Figure F-6 Flute Embouchure

EMBOUCHURE LESSON PLAN/INSTRUCTION SEQUENCE

Subject: Flute   **Grade:** 6   **Date:**

- ♪ **Concept:**
  Making a characteristic tone on the head joint

- ♪ **Behavioral Learning Objective:**
  Students will be able to form a characteristic embouchure and assess themselves or others regarding embouchure.

- ♪ **Standards:**
  MU:Pr5.3.E.5a/MU:Pr6.1.E.5a (National Standards example) or TEKS 117.208.C.3.B (State Standards example)

 **Vocabulary:** Embouchure, relaxed, pudgy

 **Materials:** Head joint

 **Time:** 10–15 minutes

27

Flute

Procedures

1. Name the parts of the head joint (embouchure hole, lip plate, etc.).

2. Students hold head joint with the open tube to their right (uncovered).

3. Have students make a blade with their hands (fingers flat and pressed together) and place it in the cleft of their chin, just touching the bottom lip.

4. Students say "pooh," pointing their attention to the shape of the lips.

5. Depending on class size:

    a. For homogenous or small classes, the teacher places the head joint for each student, has the student say "pooh," and then has them blow wind in a "pooh" syllable.

    b. For large or heterogeneous classes, the teacher has the students place their head joint and say "pooh" followed by blowing with a "pooh" syllable (emphasize using their mirror to check condensation and vertical placement).

6. Students repeat placing the head joint, blowing wind with "pooh," and evaluating their sweet spot using a mirror.

    a. For students still struggling to form condensation trails centered on the embouchure hole, use straws or paper to help them focus their wind stream.

7. Check to see if students are performing an "A" (will not be centered) on their uncovered head joint.

    a. If not, check wind speed, aperture shape, wind direction, and lastly head joint cork placement.

        i. Head joint corks can be checked with the tuning/cleaning rod by inserting the solid end of the cleaning rod (with the line) into the head joint. If the cork is correct, the line on the cleaning rod should be in the center of the embouchure hole.

ASSESSMENT

Evaluate embouchure by comparing to an ideal image of flute embouchure, check sounding pitch with a tuner (A is ideal).

REGISTER CHANGES

Unlike many of the other woodwinds, the flute lacks a mechanical method for changing registers or octaves. Instead, players use a combination of wind and fingerings to elicit higher pitches in the overtone series. A larger aperture, wind that is directed slightly lower, and a less intense wind stream leads to lower sounds, while a smaller and rounder aperture with wind directed closer to parallel to the ground and with greater intensity produces notes in the higher ranges. The majority of these changes are managed by the lips, with a little bit of wind support and jaw movement to facilitate accuracy and tone. Bringing the bottom lip forward (with a tiny bit of jaw motion) and the top lip down will make a smaller aperture of fast wind that is "raised" (closer to parallel with the floor) and will move the sound up a partial.

To assess students' apertures while playing, either have them play standing up or get down on the floor yourself to look up at their lips. This will help you identify any aperture concerns (such as shape and size) and further refine the wind stream. Beginning flutists typically start with apertures considerably larger than are necessary or desired. If directors would like to be able to provide a visual demonstration of the wind direction, the Pneumo Pro Wind Detector is a fantastic tool that uses pinwheels to show where students are directing their wind. For many of the notes in the beginner range of the instrument, fingerings will remain the same or extremely similar, and range will instead be determined primarily by aperture/wind. Using different sized straws so that students have a tactile sense of aperture size is also a great way to reinforce the necessary changes. As they begin to expand their range higher, students will also learn new fingerings to facilitate the higher harmonics.

Students can begin to practice controlling their wind once they have established consistent sweet spot placement and proper inhalation by covering the open end of the head joint. To produce a lower sound with the head joint covered, students will need to have a larger aperture and wind that is angled marginally lower than when producing uncovered sounds. Another way to help students adjust their aperture is to ask them to produce "warmer" wind, which will often be accomplished by aperture adjustment. Wind usage through these changes should remain silent, and the inhalation/exhalation expectations do not change when working with covered head joint. Once students have successfully performed the pitch A on both uncovered and covered head joints, then introduce harmonic slurs with both the covered head joint and the full instrument.

ARTICULATION

Articulation on flute relies first on appropriate use of wind and embouchure. Therefore, students should have some experience with both of these component skills before you introduce articulation. To this end, I often have my students practice "pooh" starts at the very early stages and then gradually phase in articulation with the tongue. (Pooh is *not* an articulation—it is a teaching technique to help students understand aperture shape and air regulation.) Keeping the embouchure consistent, I have beginners touch the tip of the tongue near where the upper teeth and gums meet to articulate. The tongue acts as a valve, releasing and regulating the wind as it flows into the instrument. Other teachers will often have students touch their tongue on the roof of the mouth where most people have a small ridge. (One of my students calls this the pizza burn spot, an apt descriptor in my mind.)

As students progress, their tongue placement will vary somewhat depending on both the player and the needs of the music. For instance, certain articulated styles may require variations in placement. There are many teachers who advocate tonguing between the lips, and that may be something to explore for advanced players. However, in my experience this can be a difficult approach to teach beginners in group settings.

Using syllables, although helpful for introducing the concept, can be controversial. This is largely due to differing opinions on the ideal syllable, which may in turn be because English may not have the ideal word or syllable to match ideal articulation on the flute. If using a syllable, I prefer "pooh" for beginning sounds without articulation and "too," "doo," or "thoo" when addressing articulation with young flutists. Typically, I move to mimicry rather quickly when it comes to articulation instead of sticking with syllables, and I've found that matching articulation with a good model will help many students iron out some of the idiosyncrasies on their own.

Always begin teaching articulation with connected wind and unmetered tongue movement. This allows students to concentrate on using the tip of the tongue while maintaining wind and embouchure. Remember; every time you add a new performance element or skill, students tend to struggle to maintain proficiency in the previously learned skills. After introducing the tongue motion and placement, move to metered articulation exercises. Take care to listen for tongue stops (ending/releasing the note with the tongue), as this approach can cause significant problems later in their flute journey.

ARTICULATION LESSON PLAN/INSTRUCTION SEQUENCE

Subject: Flute   **Grade:** 6   **Date:**

♪ **Concept:**
Articulating correctly on a variety of rhythms

♪ **Behavioral Learning Objective:**
Students will be able to perform articulated notes in a variety of rhythms while maintaining proper embouchure.

♪ **Standards:**
MU:Pr5.3.E.5a/MU:Pr6.1.E.5a/ MU:Pr4.2.E.5a (National Standards example) or TEKS 117.208.C.3.B (State Standards example)

 **Vocabulary:**
Articulation, tonguing, quarter notes, stability, legato

 **Materials:**
Head joint

 **Time:**
15–20 minutes

Flute

Procedures

1. Students play an A (approximation) on the head joint with the "pooh" start.
2. Students touch tongue to the back of their top teeth, near the gums.
3. Optional: Teacher models syllable (either "too" or "doo") for students and students repeat—teacher points students' attention to tongue placement.
4. Students blow wind and move their tongue without the head joint. Teacher assesses wind consistency.
5. Teacher models unmetered articulation for students.
6. Students blow wind and move their tongue with proper embouchure on head joints—unmetered practice.
7. Teacher models metered quarter notes—full value.
8. Students perform quarter notes on head joint. (Be sure to watch/listen for students who are cheating by using a breath or "who" start.)
9. Students articulate notes on the entire instrument (3rd line B).

ASSESSMENT

Assess students for connected/legato articulation and correct rhythmic performance by listening to individuals and the group.

Flute

PLAYING POSITION

There are three balance points for holding the flute: (a) the base of Finger 1, (b) RT, and (c) the lower lip against the lip plate, with the majority of the weight placed on Finger 1 and RT (Figure F-7). While exact finger placement varies, generally:

01. Left hand holds the flute between knuckle and first joint of Finger 1

02. Fingers 1, 2, and 3 curve around the instrument to rest on the keys with the ball/pad of the finger (skip one, place one, skip one, place two)

03. Left Thumb (LT) curves slight to rest on B or B-flat key

04. Right Thumb (RT) supports the flute between Fingers 4 and 5 (find a natural position on the side/pad of the thumb)

05. Right Pinky (RP) rests on the E-flat key

Fingers move from the knuckles closest to the palm and should be kept in close proximity to the keys. In terms of finger positions, two keys hold great importance to the beginning flutist. This first, the E-flat key, serves as a source of support and finger control for beginners in addition to venting to improve tone and playing E-flat. The second is the Left Thumb B/B-flat, which is one of the only keys on flute that requires shifting. Have students begin with their Left Thumb on the B key; however, later in the semester I strongly encourage directors to introduce both Left Thumb B-flat as well as either Finger 1 and 4 or chromatic/lever B-flat. I generally introduce 1 and 4/Thumb B-flat together and alternate, leaving the chromatic lever fingering until later. By forcing beginners to learn and use both fingerings from the early stages of performance, directors build solid fingering habits that accurately reflect the performance needs of more advanced music. That being said, there are debates about this topic and many skilled music educators favor one over the other with their beginners.

Flute

Figure F-7 Flute Hand Position

Many playing position problems are common to beginners. Regarding body posture, beginners are often tempted to place their right arm on the back of their chairs (particularly posture chairs due to the heights of the backs), which restricts wind usage and may impact embouchure. Furthermore, be sure to instruct students to allow their head to turn left when they bring their instrument to their lips. Outside of marching band settings, *never* insist that students perfectly square their shoulders with the instrument/head, as it restricts proper inhalation. Similarly, a marginal head tilt to the right is acceptable, provided lips and head joint remain parallel. Many beginners, however, will simply drop the flute without making the necessary head tilt.

 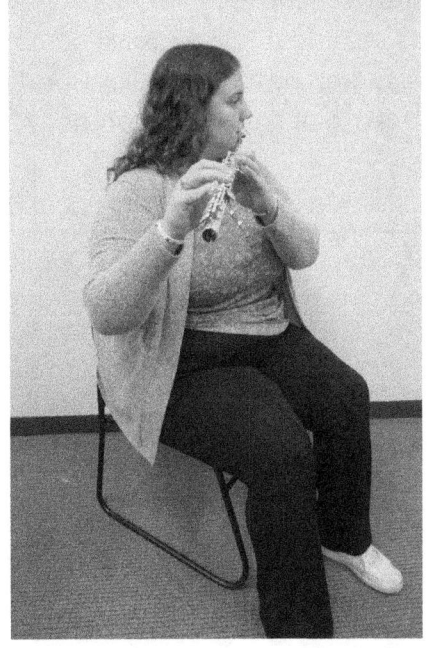

Figure F-8 Flute Playing Position

Additionally, the right wrist should be kept straight, not bent, which keeps fingers on the right hand free from tension. Bent/broken right wrists are common but significantly impact technique development and can lead to some performance injuries. Pads of the fingers should touch the keys, which is quite easy to catch on open-holed flutes where the finger pads must seal the holes. Students often reach their fingers over the keys, particularly Fingers 4, 5, and 6 (Figure F-7). Be vigilant and insist on proper embouchure/playing position, time spent on this early on may prevent many technical problems later.

Some common finger issues include:

- Left Thumb placement on the instrument body instead of B/B-flat keys
- Left Pinky hooked underneath G-sharp key
- Right Thumb misaligned (not between Fingers 4 and 5)
- Right Thumb holding the flute anywhere other than the ball of the thumb
- Right Pinky not on E-flat key
- Holding fingers straight instead of curved
- Holding fingers excessively far from the keys.

Right hand position in general should look like a backwards shaped C, with fingers relaxed and not touching the rods. If students need to raise their right elbow to maintain the proper hand position that's perfectly acceptable, but do watch for arms that drift back towards their chair instead of keeping the flute slightly in front of themselves/their neighbors.

As with all wind instruments, students should bring the instrument to the face instead of shifting the majority of their body to the instrument. For flute, it is imperative that the head joint be parallel to the lips for proper tone production. However, this may involve a compromise for younger students of a 15°–20° instrument angle with a corresponding head tilt to allow for developing right arm muscles. The most important thing is that the lips and head joint are aligned properly.

INTONATION

The head joint is the primary tuning mechanism for the flute, and the pitch center raises (**sharp**) as players push in the head joint. Conversely, pulling the head joint out makes the instrument longer and leads to a lower (flat) pitch center. Never use the head joint cork as a tuning mechanism, as that is contrary to the design of the flute and will create all sorts of intonation problems on a wide variety of notes. Remember, poor wind use and bad embouchures will not produce in-tune sounds. Therefore, wait to stress intonation until both wind and embouchures are securely developed. The flute can be tuned using the following notes:

Figure F-9 Flute Tuning Notes

Additionally, the following notes are the most egregious offenders among the notes in the standard flute range for band music.

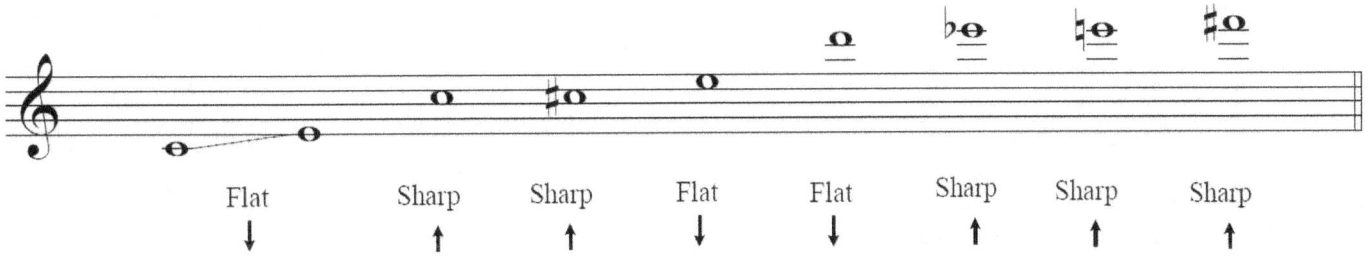

Figure F-10 Flute Intonation Challenges

Finally, dynamic changes affect tuning. With flute, the louder the sound the sharper the pitch (and conversely the softer the sound the flatter the pitch). To compensate for these tendencies, flutists make subtle changes in wind direction. During crescendos, players may direct the wind slightly downward to prevent the pitch from going sharp. Conversely, during decrescendos players may direct the wind in an increasingly parallel direction to prevent flatness.

VIBRATO

Prior to learning vibrato, students should be capable of making characteristic and centered sounds on the flute. As mentioned earlier, vibrato is a "slight variation of pitch in a sustained tone"[8] and is an essential part of flute tone production. Unlike some of the vibrato instruments, flute vibrato is created in the wind column by changes in wind pressure that pass through a relaxed chest and throat, and finally are regulated by a proper embouchure. When teaching vibrato to beginners, be careful to explain that the vibrato is *not* created through muscle movement in the mouth or jaw. I use wind pulses on the hand or with a piece of paper to give students a tactile or visual example of how the energized wind column can create vibrato. For instance, I ask my students to hold their hand in front of their mouth and blow pulses without inhaling or allowing the wind to stop completely. Some students may try to move their jaw or mouth; however, they will be unable to produce consistent pulses (which I model for the students who are struggling). The paper activity is similar, as students hold a sheet of paper in front of their mouths and blow pulses to move the paper. The goal is that the paper should move back and forth distinctly without ever coming completely to rest. Both approaches stress the importance of *slight* variations of wind intensity.

IDEAL AURAL IMAGES

1. Jean-Pierre Rampal
2. Emmanuel Pahud
3. Jeanne Baxtresser
4. Jasmine Choi
5. Severino Gazzelloni
6. Gary Schocker
7. James Galway
8. Hubert Laws
9. Fenwick Smith

SELECTED RESOURCES

Bloki Flute Method – by Bloki, published by Bloki Publishing Inc.

Trevor Wye Practice Book – by Wye, published by Novello Publishing

Flute Fundamentals: The Building Blocks of Technique – by Clardy, published by Schott

Student Instrumental Course: Flute Student Levels 1 & 2 — by Steensland and Weber, published by Alfred

---

[8] Mary Karen Clardy, *Flute Fundamentals: The Building Blocks of Technique,* Flute professor at the University of North Texas, 1993, p. 26.

Flute

BEGINNER FLUTE SEQUENCE EXAMPLE

The sequence listed below is merely a suggestion, and is not meant to be exhaustive or perfect. Instead, this sequence should serve as a leaping off point for directors to plan their own beginner courses. Also, keep in mind that many of the items, particularly at the beginning, will happen concurrently. This is, in part, because students will not have the physical or mental endurance to spend an entire class on one topic or content item. Furthermore, beginning instruction can be summed up in the phrase, "Teach, reteach, and then teach it again." Rarely will there be a class of beginners that can correctly play an instrument the first time, so directors should plan to review everything introduced several times.

1. Posture
2. Opening the case/parts of the instrument
3. Pooh and introduction to embouchure
4. Head joint placement
5. Embouchure round 2 (head joint)/first sounds
6. Introduce note symbols (rhythmic)
7. Proper hand position/how to hold the instrument
8. Long tones on head joint
9. Finger exercises
10. Note shapes/releases on head joint
11. Counting quarter note rhythms
12. Articulation (unmetered and metered) on head joint
13. Covered head joint
14. B, A, and G on the instrument (starting from 3rd space B)
15. Embouchure round 3 (uncovered and covered, working towards harmonic slurs)
16. Low-high-low (harmonic slurs on covered head joint)
17. Learn rote songs (mi-re-do)
18. Counting quarter/half/whole note rhythms
19. The staff and reading B, A, and G (include singering, see chapter 4)
20. D, E-flat, and F on the instrument (starting from 4th line D)
21. Learn rote songs (sol-mi, sol-mi-do)
22. Reading F, E, and D (including singering—see chapter 4)
23. Begin method book work
24. B-flat (3rd space, both fingerings), C-sharp (3rd space), and E (4th space) on the instrument
25. Octave slurs starting on low F
26. Reading/sight-reading in the method book (add fingerings as needed)
27. Scales using tetrachords
28. Head joint harmonics, add second partial
29. More reading and technical finger passages
30. One-octave scales
31. Vibrato
32. Harmonics on the flute
33. Two/three octave major scales, minor scales, further technique exercises

Flute

PRACTICAL TIPS

Assembly

- ♪ Know the ways to tell if the case is right side up or upside down.
    - ⊙ Manufacturer label on top
    - ⊙ Latches may open up
    - ⊙ Top may be thinner
    - ⊙ Handle may be on bottom
- ♪ Always open the case on the floor.
- ♪ Clean the tenons regularly.
- ♪ Don't grab the rods.
- ♪ Rod on the foot joint lines up with keys on the body.
- ♪ Embouchure hole lines up with keys on the body.

Breathing

- ♪ Flute requires the largest volume of wind.
- ♪ Inhalation is where the majority of muscular effort happens; students must breathe in deeply.
- ♪ (Relatively) quiet inhalations are without tension.
- ♪ Breathe to play, not to live (they aren't the same).
- ♪ The lungs have greater capacity than students tend to think.
- ♪ Wind use is regulated at the lips via the aperture, students with apertures that are too large will struggle to hold long notes.

Embouchure

- ♪ Keep wind speed constant; the embouchure needs to form around wind.
- ♪ Air direction matters.
  - ⊙ Lips must direct wind across and down.
- ♪ **Sweet spot** placement will depend on the shape of the lips (both top and bottom).
  - ⊙ Full bottom lips generally have a sweet spot that is often *slightly* higher on the face.
  - ⊙ Thin bottom lips generally have a sweet spot that is often *slightly* lower on the face.
  - ⊙ Tear drops and Cupid's bows on the top lips make controlling the air direction more difficult.
    - Students can still play with tear drops/Cupid's bows, but their sweet spot will often be off-center on their lips/not aligned with their nose, or they will have to move their top lip to remove the obstruction.
  - ⊙ Use the cleft of the chin as a guide for head joint placement.
  - ⊙ Rolling in/out should be used to find the right bottom lip covering, never for intonation with beginners.
  - ⊙ Check sweet spot placement via vapor trail/condensation. (Does it line up with the embouchure hole?)
  - ⊙ Place head joints the first time for the students.
  - ⊙ Sweet spot must stay the same when playing on the entire instrument.
- ♪ Relaxed/sad/down—Have words to help students keep tension out of their bottom lip.
- ♪ Help students find their sweet spot.

- Make students use a mirror—the flute has less tactile feedback in the embouchure than other instruments.
- Don't press the head joint up against the lips too hard.
- The lips should come forward towards the flute/lip plate.
- Bottom lip covers 1/4 TO 1/3 of the embouchure hole.
- Bottom lip must remain soft/pudgy.
- Beginners tend to have apertures that are too large.
- Corners come in and down, not back and up.
- Flexibility, especially in corners, is necessary for register changes.
- Students' heads shouldn't move as part of forming an embouchure.
- Teeth either even or in an overbite may make first sounds easier.
- "Pooh" or "pure" to get the aperture/embouchure shape.
  - Neither syllable is an articulation.
- Good tone for beginners depends on correct sweet spot (alignment of embouchure hole and wind stream, i.e., head joint placement) and embouchure shape supported by good wind use, which leads to the right wind stream hitting the right place on the head joint to produce an edge tone.
- Small and circular aperture = high notes; oval shaped and slightly larger aperture = low notes.
- Corners energize in more as the notes go higher, jaw will move *slightly* for octave shift.
- Be willing to do head joint practice for quite some time.

Articulation

- Proper wind, sweet spot placement, and embouchure are necessary for articulation; do not teach articulation until these are relatively well established.
- Wind flows out when playing, in when breathing only. Articulation is more like waving a hand across an open faucet of water; the water never stops nor should the wind.
- Generally, tongues that touch too low (between teeth/against bottom teeth) or too high (back on the roof of the mouth) will inhibit connected and quick articulation.
  - They also tend to sound heavy/thunky.
- Tongue stops should be avoided with beginners at all costs.

Playing Position

- Right hand comes slightly forward.
- Head turns slightly to the left.
  - Head/shoulders/knees should *not* be in alignment for beginners.
- Right wrist should be relatively in alignment with right arm (avoid significantly broken wrists).
- Sweet spot placement requires reps.
  - Lots and lots of reps
- Practice moving fingers while holding the instrument (no playing).
  - Both one at a time and in patterns
- Curved fingers are **crucial** to future technique.
  - Fingers cover holes and only touch keys
- Flutes are balanced, not gripped.
  - Left thumb = comfortably placed on the B natural key
  - Right thumb mostly perpendicular to flute (balance point)
    - Check this often as it leads to significant technical issues in the right hand when held incorrectly.
  - Left knuckle balance point will push the head joint *slightly* into the bottom lip/chin.

Other Tips

- Shoot for concert A on the open head joint. It will not be centered/in tune initially
  - Check crown/cork positions and keep students from playing with the crown.
- Wind speed should be partially regulated by aperture size (i.e., support with wind at all times).
- Embouchure and wind direction/speed address register changes and a significant portion of intonation.
- Have the goal of resonant sounds, even on the head joint.
- Once students can accurately perform them, make octave slurs/harmonic exercises a crucial part of their practice.

Flute

- Good technique requires proper hand position (balance, not grip).
- Practice finger patterns to give faces a break early in the year.
- Woodwind technique is largely making students do a large variety of technical patterns a ridiculous number of times.
- Not all octaves have the same fingerings for the same notes.
- Force correct repetitions of difficult finger combinations.
  - Proper uses of B-flat fingerings
  - Pinkies
  - C/C-sharp/D
- Piccolo
  - Avoid pressing the instrument into the lips with excessive force.
    - Use enough pressure to anchor the balance point, but it shouldn't hurt or .distort the bottom lip beyond the ability to make changing octaves hard

- Sweet spot placement will be higher on the lower lip for many students—especially if the instrument doesn't have a lip plate.

- The aperture is smaller, but not so small that players buzz/vibrate.

- Pitch tendencies can vary wildly between instrument makes and models.

- Wind support and fast air are needed to keep from playing flat.

- Players often cover more of the embouchure hole/roll in more on piccolo than they do on flute—but this isn't always the case.

- Finger technique may be made more challenging by excessively compact keywork/fingerings. Keep this in mind for student with larger hands/longer fingers.

- Be prepared to use alternative fingerings more often for response and intonation issues.

- Generally, hold the instrument parallel to the ground.

- Mistakes in embouchure, aperture, hand position, etc. are magnified by the piccolo.

- Shrill, sharp sounds are often due to a small oral cavity or air that is aimed too high.

- Scoops often come from a lack of wind support.

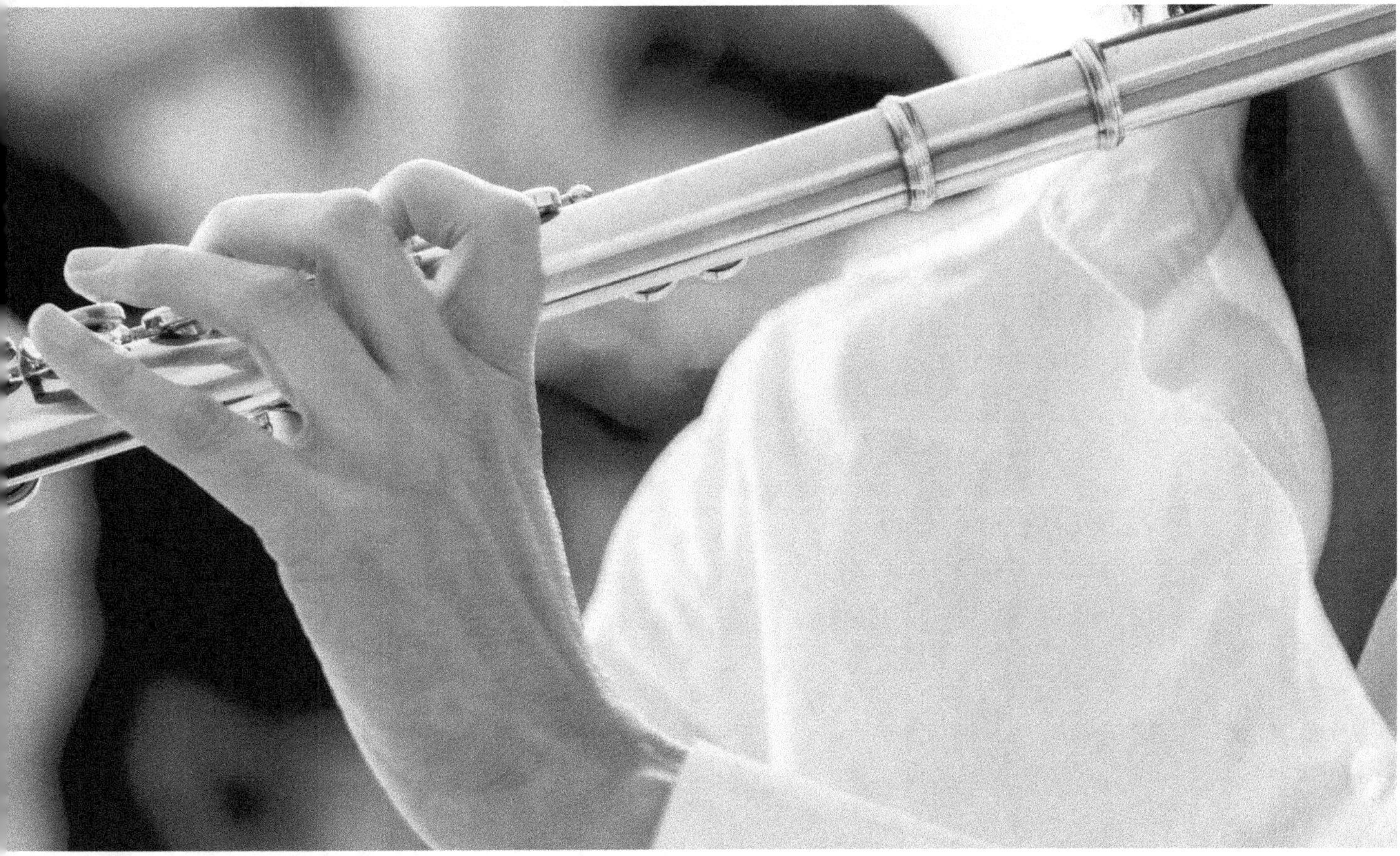

TROUBLESHOOTING FLUTE

Problem	Possible Causes	Possible Solutions
Small/Weak Tone	⊙ Lack of wind support/poor use of wind ⊙ Poor head joint placement ⊙ Aperture too small ⊙ Closed Throat	⊙ Larger inhalation, relax/open throat/slightly increase aperture ⊙ Fix off-centered embouchure hole/lip plate may need to be higher on lips/keep chin and head level ⊙ Open the aperture to the correct size (no larger than embouchure hole) ⊙ Relax the tongue/throat to create a more open oral cavity.

Unfocused tone	⊙ Wind direction
	⊙ Aperture size
	⊙ Lower lip placement
		⊙ Angle wind across and down over the center of the embouchure hole
		⊙ Decrease aperture size
		⊙ Adjust the amount of lower lip covering the hole
		   • Too much lip = fuzz and flat
		   • Too little lip = bright and sharp

Fuzzy, Flat Tone	⊙ Wind direction ⊙ Aperture size and placement	⊙ Keep chin up/roll head joint out ⊙ Smaller/rounder aperture in the sweet spot
Shrill, Sharp Tone	⊙ Wind intensity ⊙ Aperture size	⊙ Less wind intensity ⊙ Larger aperture
Heavy Articulation	⊙ Too much tongue pressure on teeth ⊙ Too much wind pressure behind tongue ⊙ Tongue touches too low/between teeth	⊙ Use less tongue pressure/only use the tip tongue ⊙ Less intense wind pressure ⊙ Move the contact point higher inside the mouth
Scoop/Dip Sound	⊙ Too much movement (jaw/tongue)	⊙ Jaw movement is unnecessary for flute/use the tip of the tongue

Flute

Poor Accents	<ul><li>Split pitches when accenting</li><li>Not enough accent</li></ul>	<ul><li>Control wind speed at the beginning of notes</li><li>Increase wind pressure at the beginning of the note</li></ul>
Poor Staccato	<ul><li>Lack of wind support</li></ul>	<ul><li>Provide more wind support</li></ul>
Sluggish Articulation	<ul><li>Moving too much tongue</li><li>Tonguing between the teeth</li><li>Overblowing</li></ul>	<ul><li>Use less tongue/only use tip</li><li>Move contact point higher inside the mouth</li><li>Control wind speed/intensity</li></ul>
Difficulty Changing Ranges	<ul><li>Lack of aperture/wind control</li></ul>	<ul><li>Use overtone/harmonic exercises to increase controls</li></ul>
Sharp Pitch	<ul><li>Head joint pushed in too far</li><li>Aperture too small/narrow/uncentered</li><li>Overblowing</li><li>Wind stream angled too high/parallel to the floor</li><li>Not enough lip covering the embouchure hole</li><li>Instrument position</li></ul>	<ul><li>Pull out head joint</li><li>Increase aperture size</li><li>Control wind speed</li><li>Lower wind stream (slightly)</li><li>Cover more of the embouchure hole</li><li>Adjust instrument so that head joint is parallel to lips and embouchure hole is correct (not rolled out)</li></ul>
Flat Pitch	<ul><li>Head joint pulled too far</li><li>Aperture too large/wide/uncentered</li><li>Lack of wind support</li><li>Wind stream directed too far down</li><li>Too much lip covering embouchure hole</li><li>Instrument position</li></ul>	<ul><li>Push in head joint</li><li>Correct aperture size/shape/placement</li><li>Increase wind support</li><li>Raise wind stream (slightly)</li><li>Cover less of the embouchure hole</li><li>Adjust instrument so that head joint is parallel to lips and embouchure hole is correct (not rolled in)</li></ul>

FLUTE FINGERINGS

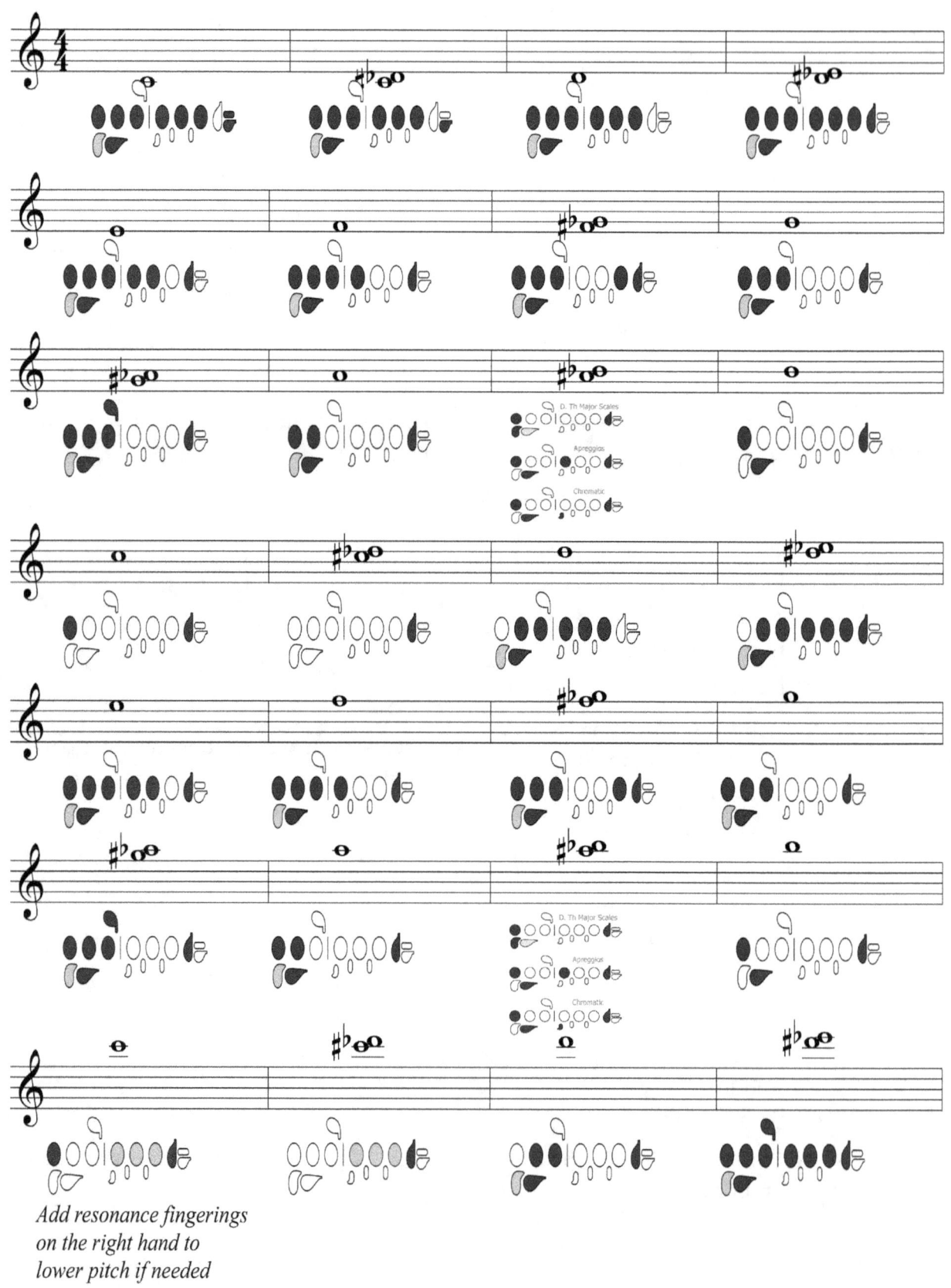

Add resonance fingerings on the right hand to lower pitch if needed

FLUTE FINGERINGS

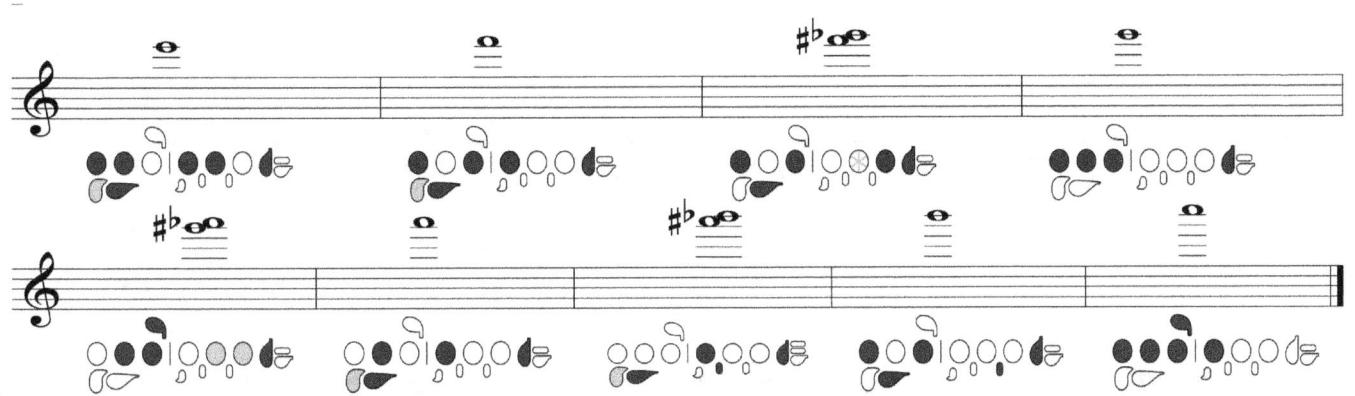

Add resonance fingerings on the right hand to lower pitch if needed

FLUTE SUPPLEMENTAL EXERCISES

FLUTE SUPPLEMENTAL EXERCISES

FLUTE SUPPLEMENTAL EXERCISES

FLUTE SUPPLEMENTAL EXERCISES

© 2025 Agogic Press

Agogic Press grants permission to duplicate this worksheet for non-profit, educational use only, provided each copy includes this copyright notice.
Copies may not be sold or included in any materials offered for sale or for any form of profit.

FLUTE SUPPLEMENTAL EXERCISES

FLUTE SUPPLEMENTAL EXERCISES

DOUBLE REEDS

For many band directors, double reeds can be intimidating mysteries. Both oboe and bassoon, however, can add wonderful tone colors to an ensemble. The most important general topic of discussion for understanding double reeds are the reeds themselves.

All double reeds have blades, which are two cut sections of cane that create an oval tip opening. Similar to single reeds, the nature of the tip opening influences the sound, and high-quality reeds will vibrate evenly across the tip. To facilitate vibration, reeds should be soaked for a few minutes in room temperature water whenever possible. Do not wet reeds with saliva, as that will shorten the lifespan of the reed and the pressure of teeth or lips may change the overall reed shape.

There is a valid reason why double reed players obsess over the quality of their reeds. More than other woodwinds, for whom reed quality is already important, the reed is the primary determiner of tone and intonation for oboists and bassoonists. Therefore, having quality reeds is absolutely necessary for a quality performance. If directors chose to start double reed players (and personally I have had success starting both oboists and bassoonists at the same time as other instruments) then providing quality reeds is a must. Some companies sell handmade reeds over the internet, which can facilitate reed purchases if private lesson staff on the instruments are not available. Reeds themselves are tuned and should be cut and trimmed to specific instruments and players by an expert whenever possible.

Good reeds respond freely and easily, play relatively well in tune across the instrument, facilitate dynamics and articulations of all kinds, and provide appropriate backpressure. When evaluating reeds, there are several important considerations. The winding/binding should be even and neat, providing a tight and stable fit for the reed. Additionally, the cane should have an off-yellow color; green sheen or brown streaks in the lay indicate poor cane quality. Symmetry is very important in double reeds, particularly regarding the cut of the lay (quality heart, channels and rails). Reeds that have an even, symmetrical, smooth lay are more likely to produce quality sounds and respond to student wind consistently. Correspondingly, the tip of the reed should also be even across both blades. Finally, on bassoon, the first and second wires should fit tightly around the entire reed, as they are responsible for shaping the reed in addition to holding the blades together. Oboe reeds should crow (the double buzz sound made by double reeds) around C and buzz around G, while bassoon reeds should crow between E-flat and F and buzz around E.

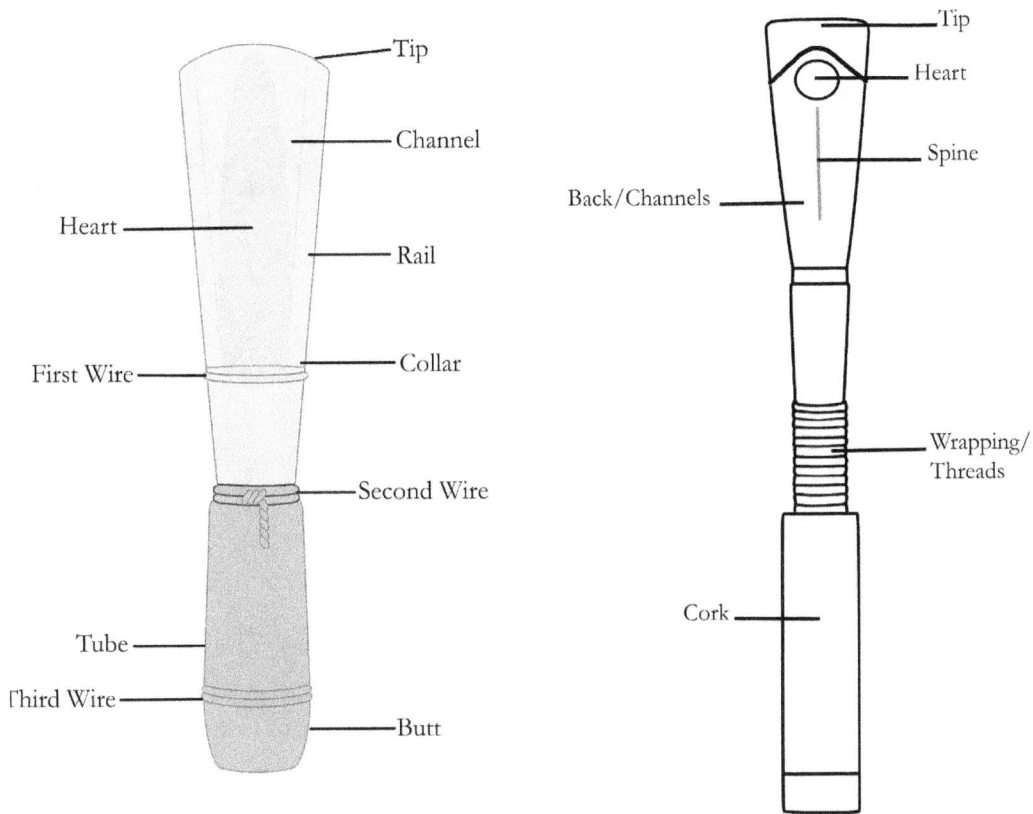

Figures D-1 and D-2 Oboe and Bassoon Reeds

If directors wish to learn reed making/care themselves, I strongly suggest they first purchase a reed kit. Secondly, find someone from whom they can take lessons, as this is the most effective way to learn reed making. While there are some texts, both general[9] and specific[10] with solid guides for adjusting reeds, personal instruction makes a considerable difference in developing the skills to effectively create or adjust double reeds. It also takes time, materials, and a willingness to make mistakes. Only embark on this path if you are committed to the journey.

To this end, I would not recommend starting oboists and bassoonists in one large heterogeneous class setting without some kind of private lesson teacher support, if for no other reason than the reeds themselves. Beginners require considerable help in learning how to handle their reeds and instruments (which are easily knocked out of adjustment). Furthermore, both reeds and instruments bring with them some of the highest replacement/repair costs of any of the instruments in band. Therefore, providing proper instruction in large heterogeneous classes can be quite challenging, and in general, instruction and pacing at the beginning will be slower than many other woodwinds.

---

9   Ely and Van Deuren, *Wind Talk for Woodwinds*; Westphal, *Guide to Teaching Woodwinds*. Both of these are excellent reference books for woodwind information.
10 Goossens and Roxburgh, *Oboe*; Spencer, *The Art of Bassoon Playing*; Sprenkle and Ledet, *The Art of Oboe Playing*

OBOE

Oboe

Along with the flute and trombone, the oboe dates back to ancient times. The modern oboe first appeared on the musical scene in the late 1650s and was open holed without an octave key. Over the years both key mechanisms and the two octave keys common today were added, and the version of the oboe used today was in production by the early twentieth century. While there are technically four members of the oboe family (oboe, English horn, Oboe d'amore, and bass oboe), most band directors will only work with the oboe and English horn. Fingerings on the two instruments are nearly identical, and they share the same written range. The oboe is a C instrument (non-transposing) and notation for oboe is written in the sounding range (Figure O-1).

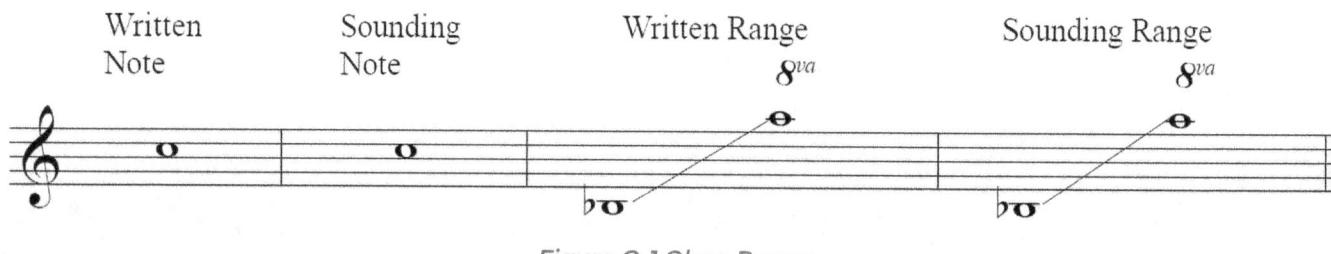

Figure O-1 Oboe Range

While not rigid, below are approximate beginner, intermediate, and advanced ranges.

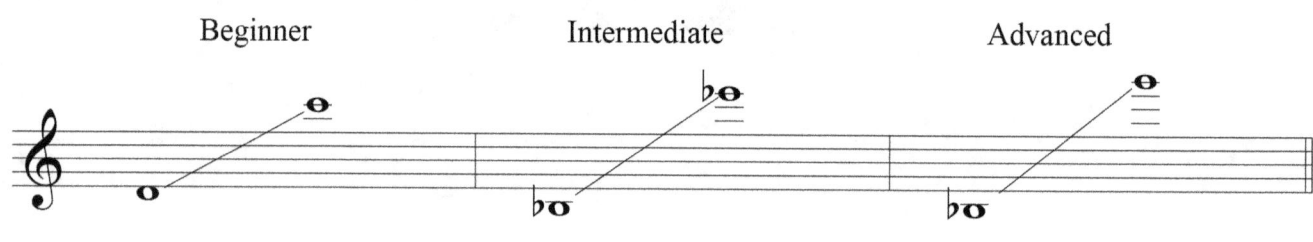

Figure O-2 Oboe Skill Range

The English horn, however, is an F transposing instrument and sounds a 5th lower than written (Figure O-3).

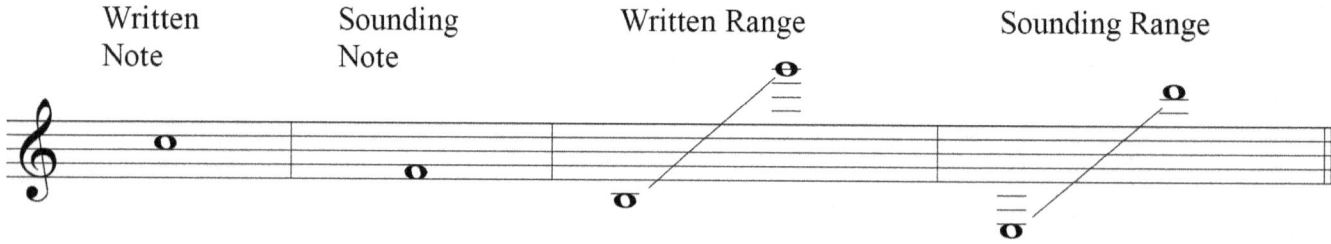

Figure O-3 English Horn Range

INSTRUMENT SELECTION

If oboe is a beginner instrument in the program, student selection is a critical task for the band director. Due to the delicate nature of the instrument, students who have shown responsibility and the ability to follow directions are good fits for oboe. Directors may measure this through individual experiences with the student or through references from other teachers. Prior musical training is also something to watch for, as the jump-start in listening skills may be meaningful. Finally, an under bite, or protruding lower jaw, may inhibit embouchure development, particularly in the beginning stages.

EQUIPMENT

Oboes are often school-owned instruments and selecting appropriate equipment can be daunting for non-oboists. Below are some suggestions, chosen at the time of publication, that may change due to model updates and manufacturer quality. Additionally, do not hesitate to ask other band directors or private instructors for their recommendations. Intermediate and professional oboes are often made of wood, typically grenadilla; however, reasonable quality resin oboes exist. Resin models work well for beginners, and high school students will certainly benefit from the improved tone quality of the wood instruments. I recommend these resin options for beginners due to their durability and consistency.

INSTRUMENT

Fox Model 300, Renard Artist Model 330, Renard Protege Model 333, Tiery J10 and E30

Obtaining quality reeds is the most important equipment consideration for working with young oboists. If possible, I would suggest starting with a private instructor or professional player in your area. If there are no oboists around to craft reeds for students, online options are available. Know that any online reeds will need adjustment to match both the player and instrument.

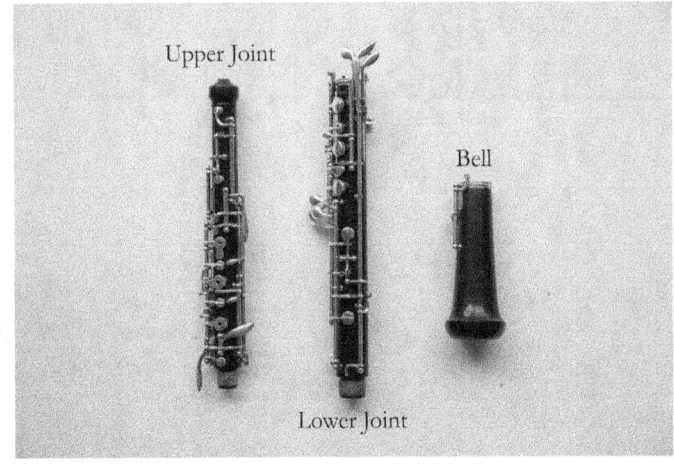

Figure O-4 Oboe Parts

ASSEMBLY

Because oboe is one of the easiest instruments for students to damage, directors should take the time to instruct students in detail regarding assembly and handling. Before putting the instrument together, be sure to address opening the case, naming the parts of the instrument, and handling reeds. Additionally, point out the 2-3 bridge keys to the students prior to their first attempt at putting the instrument together. Once students have a clear understanding of the instrument parts and how to handle them, teach assembly by starting with putting the bell on the lower joint. The bell slides on the exposed cork at the bottom of the lower joint. Students should hold the bell with the left hand and press the key to lift the bridge as they gently twist the bell onto the instrument, lining up the necessary bridge key.

After students have correctly assembled the bell and lower joint, have them hold the upper joint so that the bridge keys stay open and align these keys with their counterparts on the lower joint. With a small, gentle twist and some pressure, slide the upper joint into the lower joint. Take note to keep the twisting motion quite small, as there is little wiggle room before the bridge keys will come into contact with other parts of the instrument. New tenon corks often need greasing, and students can place a small amount of cork grease on the corks, rub the grease into the corks, and then assemble the instrument. Over time, the need for greasing the corks will subside, and students will not need to put grease on every time.

Finally, insert the reed completely into the top of the upper joint, with no space left at the bottom of the reed cork. Some corks may be the wrong size for the opening in the top of the upper joint. Corks that are too large may need to be sanded slightly and directors should be very cautious in order to not sand off too much and break the seal. If cork sanding is necessary, make small adjustments and check the fit often.

Figure O-5 Oboe Assembly

TONE PRODUCTION AND EMBOUCHURE

After wind use, embouchure is the next core component of tone production, and in the case of the oboe, the primary purpose of the embouchure is to facilitate proper reed vibration. To that end, embouchure cannot overcome a poor reed; regularly check student reeds for quality (warping, chipping, etc.). Oboe reeds consist of two main sections: the blades and the staple. The blades contain the cut/lay of the reed where the primary vibration takes place and the staple holds the winding/binding and the cork. Reed tips, or the thin end of the reed, contain the oval tip opening. Furthermore, the heart, as in single reeds, is the center point of the reed that controls the basic vibration. In the case of oboe reeds, the heart may not be visible when held to the light depending on the cut of the reed. This does not mean that the reed lacks a heart; rather, evaluating the heart is more complicated contingent on the manner in which the reed was created.

Reeds must be soaked in fresh water, and oboists should have a small cup or container with them for that purpose. Never get the cork wet on an oboe reed; instead, only submerge the blades of the reed in water. Varying opinions exist about how long to soak the reeds, which is made more complicated by the variability of the reeds themselves. Generally speaking, the blades should be wet enough to seal on the sides/corners and to vibrate freely—something that, in my opinion, often takes only a few minutes (2–3 being common).

Both lips cover teeth in double reed embouchures. Students should drop their jaw slightly and place the reed on the center of their bottom lip, rolled slightly over the teeth. With the top lip similarly covering the top teeth, students should then bring their lips together. Finally, students should create a seal by energizing the corners inward towards the reed. When sealing the reed, students should keep the center of the lips round and avoid biting with their teeth. Those with thin lips may need to roll more of their lips over their teeth to provide the necessary support for reed vibration, and thick-lipped student may not need as much lip inside their mouth. Biting with the teeth is not necessary, and in fact will often close the tip opening so much that sound production becomes impossible. The lips hold and support the reed, not the teeth.

Even in the best circumstances, the size of the tip opening on oboe reeds creates an enormous amount of backpressure; therefore, directors must develop corner muscle strength incrementally in beginners. Moreover, players will need to exhale bad wind at times prior to new inhalations. All of this backpressure can lead to biting with the jaw or tension in the throat or tongue, and directors should watch for unwanted tension in beginners. A properly developed embouchure with good wind support and a quality reed should not produce tension in performers.

One quick note: newer reeds need less time soaking in water than older reeds. While a new reed may only need 30-60 seconds to open properly, older reeds may need as long as 2-3 minutes in water so that they open up.

Oboe

Figure O-6 Oboe Embouchure

EMBOUCHURE LESSON PLAN/INSTRUCTIONAL SEQUENCE

Subject: Oboe   **Grade:** 6   **Date:**

♪ **Concept:**
Making a characteristic tone on the reed

♪ **Behavioral Learning Objective:**
Students will be able to form a characteristic embouchure and assess themselves or others regarding embouchure.

♪ **Standards:**
MU:Pr5.3.E.5a/MU:Pr6.1.E.5a (National Standards example) or TEKS 117.208.C.3.B (State Standards example)

Vocabulary:
Embouchure, energize, lips, teeth

Materials:
Reed

Time:
10–15 minutes

Oboe

Procedures

1. Students open the jaw and make an "oh" or whistle shape with their lips.
2. Student curl their lips slightly over their teeth.
3. Student place the tip of their pinky finger on the center of the bottom lip, at least past their fingernail.
4. Students bring the top lip down to touch their finger (top teeth do not touch).
5. Students energize the corners of their mouth to seal around their finger, as in saying "ooo."

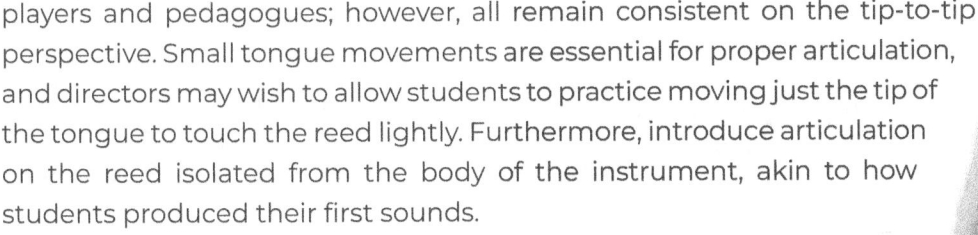

ASSESSMENT
Evaluate embouchure by comparing to an ideal image of oboe embouchure, check sounding pitch with a tuner. (C is ideal.)

ARTICULATION

Like all wind instruments, proper wind support is necessary for correct articulation. Similar to other reed instruments, oboists use the tip of the tongue to articulate by touching the tip of the tongue to the tip of the reed. The specific tonguing location and syllable used often differ between players and pedagogues; however, all remain consistent on the tip-to-tip perspective. Small tongue movements are essential for proper articulation, and directors may wish to allow students to practice moving just the tip of the tongue to touch the reed lightly. Furthermore, introduce articulation on the reed isolated from the body of the instrument, akin to how students produced their first sounds.

Oboe

ARTICULATION LESSON PLAN

Subject: Oboe **Grade:** 6 **Date:**

♪ **Concept:**
Articulating correctly on a variety of rhythms

♪ **Behavioral Learning Objective:**
Students will be able to perform articulated notes in a variety of rhythms while maintaining proper embouchure.

♪ **Standards:**
MU:Pr5.3.E.5a/MU:Pr6.1.E.5a/ MU:Pr4.2.E.5a (National Standards example) or TEKS 117.208.C.3.B (State Standards example)

Vocabulary:
Articulation, tonguing, quarter notes, stability, legato.

Materials:
Mouthpiece, neck, reed, ligature, white/chalk board, entire instrument (optional).

Time:
15–20 minutes

Procedures

1. Students crow on the reed to review embouchure and wind use.
2. Students touch top of the tip of the tongue to the bottom of the tip of the reed.
3. Optional: Teacher models articulation sound for students.
4. Students blow wind and move their tongue without the reed—teacher assesses wind consistency.
5. Teacher models unmetered articulation for students.
6. Students blow wind and move their tongue with proper embouchure on reed—unmetered practice.
7. Teacher models metered quarter notes—full value.
8. Students perform quarter notes on reed. (Be sure to watch/listen for students who are cheating by using a breath or "who" start.)
9. Optional: Students articulate notes on the entire instrument.

ASSESSMENT

Assess students for connected/legato articulation and correct rhythmic performance by listening to individuals and the group.

PLAYING POSITION

The angle the reed enters the mouth will greatly impact control, and students should seek to have an even balance between top and bottom lips on the reed. Therefore, students should hold the oboe at approximately a 35°–45° angle, which is slightly closer to parallel with the floor when compared to the clarinet. Furthermore, students' heads should stay in alignment with the spine, and chins should not drop down towards the chest, as both actions will create an imbalance in the embouchure. Individual variations in instrument angle are due to teeth and lip shape, and students should always hold their instrument at the angle that produces the best sound across all registers.

The right thumb provides the majority of support when playing the oboe, however the embouchure and left thumb way also serve as balance points. When instructing playing position, take great care to assure that the right thumb is in the correct position (thumb pad under the thumb rest and pointing towards the body of the instrument). Many young oboists slide their right thumb too far under the thumb rest, which can create instability for the instrument and pain for the students.

Figure O-7 Oboe Playing Position

INTONATION

The oboe is a fantastic instrument to use for pitch reference when performed with a proper embouchure and correct wind support on a tuned reed combined with a well-adjusted instrument held at the proper angle with the correct amount of reed in the mouth in rooms with appropriate temperature and humidity. It is no wonder, with all the qualifiers in the previous sentence, that oboe intonation drives so many band directors to madness. Therefore, do not rely on oboists to provide pitch reference until they have progressed to the point where they can consistently play in tune. Otherwise, you are setting both yourself and your student up for frustration.

With all of that in mind, intonation starts with the quality of the reed. Unlike many of the other instruments, oboe does not have an easy way to adjust pitch mechanically. As we discussed earlier, reeds must be tuned (often to A = 440) on each particular instrument and oboe reeds that are relatively in tune will generally crow a B or C. Reeds can be scrapped to make adjustments in intonation, but this should be done by someone with reed making experience. The specific pitch will matter more to the reed maker, but shooting for B/C is a good rule of thumb.

The oboe can be tuned using the following notes:

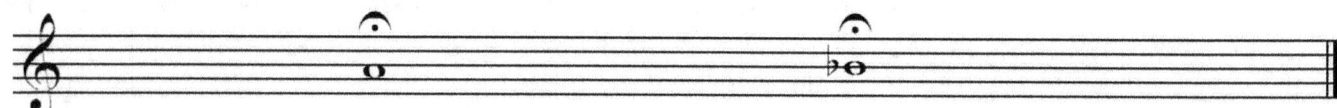

Figure O-8 Oboe Tuning Notes

Additionally, the following notes are the most egregious offenders among the notes in the standard oboe range for band music.

Problem Notes on Oboe

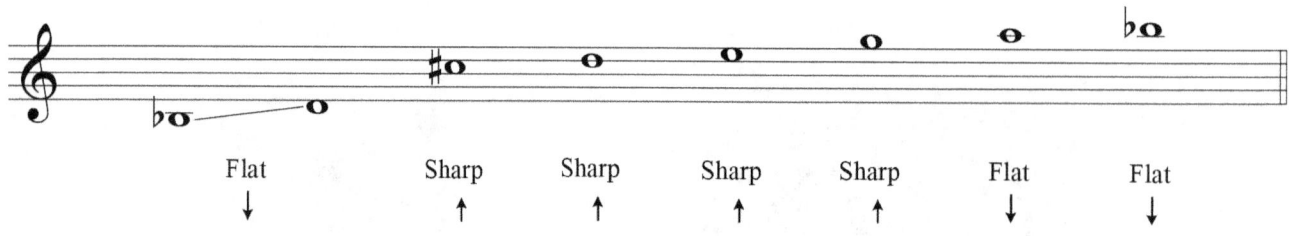

Figure O-9 Oboe Intonation Challenges

Once reed quality is established, several other factors affect oboe intonation. If the pad openings are too small or too large, or the instrument is generally out of adjustment, intonation will suffer. Also, playing position influences pitch in addition to tone. If students hold the oboe at too great an angle (> 45°) then the overall pitch will be flat. Conversely, if the instrument is held too close to the body (< 45°) then the oboe will be sharp. Furthermore, reed placement has a strong impact on pitch, where too much reed in the mouth can greatly raise the pitch and too little will produce noticeably flat sounds. Reed placement will also impact tone quality, so I suggest being cautious when asking players to adjust pitch this way to avoid sacrificing timbre for intonation. Finally, the oboe tends to go sharp during crescendos and flat during decrescendos.

DYNAMICS

Dynamics are extremely difficult for young oboists to control, and many a band director has been frustrated with the piercing timbre/volume combination common among beginners. This frustration, and the feedback that it elicits, can often lead to biting or a lack of wind support simply to make other students or the teacher happy. Accept that beginning oboe is a loud, piercing instrument until students have developed the embouchure and wind control necessary to make softer sounds and stay *in tone/tune*. The reason for this is that pesky wind backpressure, since oboe reeds require constant and relatively consistent embouchure/wind pressure to produce quality tones. When teaching students to play soft (after they have demonstrated appropriate embouchure/wind maturity) directors should address specific mechanics needed for control. For instance, to play soft wind volume must decrease while wind speed increases. To control the wind effectively, the aperture size must decrease in addition to the change in wind, which is why both embouchure and wind should be somewhat controlled before introducing dynamic variation to beginning oboists.

VIBRATO

Oboe is also a vibrato instrument, and one where the mechanism for producing vibrato is hotly debated. Some pedagogues are strong proponents of diaphragmatic vibrato[11] while others argue for changes in wind pressure in the throat.[12] In either case, vibrato is **NOT** produced by moving the jaw or lips unless directors desire frequent squeaks from the oboe section. I encourage those interested in the finer points of oboe vibrato to seek more information from the cited sources.

---

11   Goossens & Roxburgh, *Oboe*, 1993; Rothwell, *Oboe Technique*, 1983; Sprenkle & Ledet, *The Art of Oboe Playing: Including Problems and Techniques of Oboe Reedmaking*, 1961.

12   Schuring, *Oboe Art and Method*, 2009.

Oboe

SPECIAL TECHNIQUES

Half-hole is the term used to describe when an oboist rolls their first finger (Finger 1) down and vents through the vent hole and is used for the notes shown below:

Two considerations should be given to using the half-hole: rolling and hand/finger position. Students should roll their first finger and not slide it down on the extension plate. First, making this motion correctly will keep the key depressed while minimizing the amount of movement/distance the first finger travels, thus allowing for a quick return to the home position. Significant repetition is necessary for students to automatize their half-hole motion and directors should include exercises for any unusual finger movements on any woodwind instrument.

Second, the hand position and remaining fingers must stay in their home positions. Students desperately want to adjust the rest of their hand to accommodate the roll for the half-hole, therefore directors need to watch carefully for fingers that lift away from the keys or hands/wrists that collapse.

Intermediate and professional model oboes have three distinct fingerings for F with generally agreed-upon rules for their usage. The two most common fingering are often labeled as standard/regular and left F.

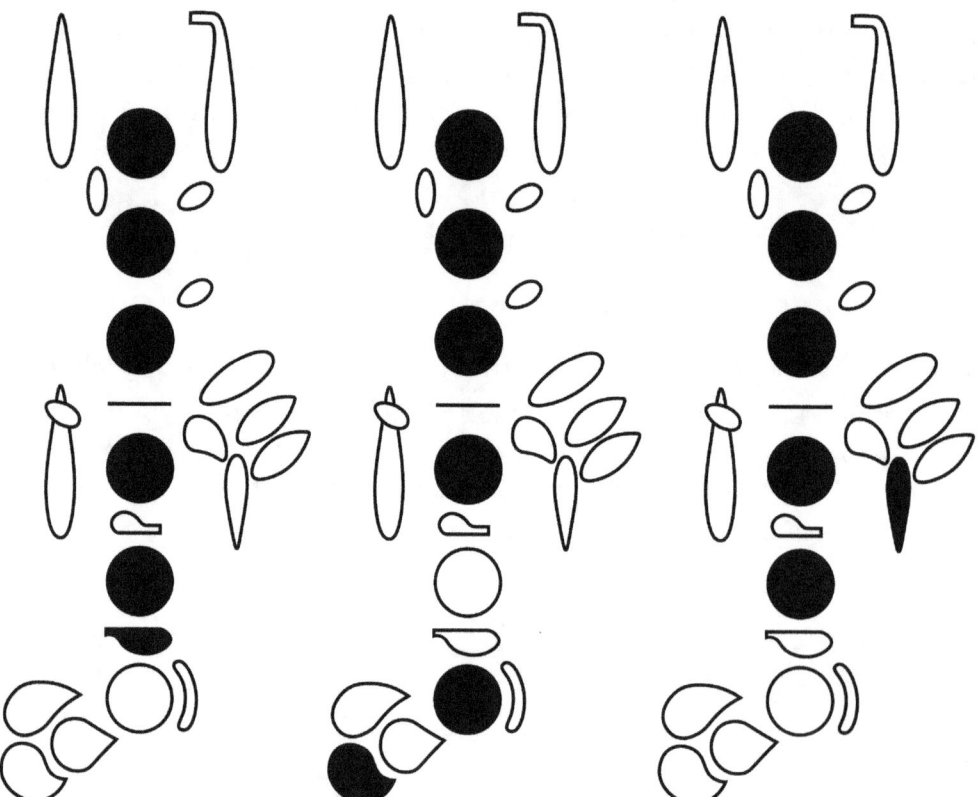

Figure O-10 Oboe F Fingerings

Oboe

Not all student models come with a left F key. Therefore, forked F can be used when necessary to avoid the awkward finger problems normally addressed by left F, such as transitioning from D to F. In my opinion, beginners should know *at least* two F fingerings and be forced to practice them both so that they build muscle memory for avoiding future technique problems.

IDEAL AURAL IMAGES

1. Lian Wang
2. Heinz Hollinger
3. Albrech Mayer
4. Elaine Douvas
5. Nick Stovall
6. Eugene Izotov
7. Ariana Ghez
8. John Ferrillo
9. Alex Klein

SELECTED BEGINNER REPERTOIRE

Bocal Majority's Beginner Boot Camp Books (my favorite) – by Bohls and Auerbach, published Bocal Majority Woodwinds

Rubank Elementary Method for Oboe – by Hovey, published by Hal Leonard

Learn to Play Oboe, Bk 1: A Carefully Graded Method That Develops Well-Rounded Musicianship – by MacBeth, published by Alfred

BEGINNER OBOE SEQUENCE EXAMPLE

The sequence listed below is merely a suggestion and is not meant to be exhaustive or perfect. Instead, this sequence should serve as a leaping-off point for directors to plan their own beginner courses. Also, keep in mind that many of the items, particularly at the beginning, will happen concurrently. This is due, in part, to the fact that students will not have the physical or mental endurance to spend an entire class on one topic or content item. Furthermore, beginning instruction can be summed up in the phrase, "Teach, reteach, and then teach it again." Rarely will there be a class of beginners that understand and can correctly play an instrument the first time, so plan to review everything you introduce.

1. Breathing
2. Posture
3. Opening the case/parts of the instrument/care of the instrument
4. Embouchure (using thumb)

69

5. Proper hand position/how to hold the instrument
6. Embouchure round 2 (on reed)/first sounds
7. Finger exercises
8. Introduce note symbols (rhythmic)
9. Long tones on reed
10. Note shapes/releases
11. Counting quarter note rhythms
12. Articulation (unmetered and metered)
13. Reed to full instrument sounds
14. C, B, A, and G on the instrument (starting on 3rd space C)
15. Embouchure round 3 (reed checking crow pitch at B-C)
16. Learn rote songs (mi-re-do)
17. Counting quarter/half/whole note rhythms
18. The staff and reading B, A, and G (include singing)
19. F-sharp, F, E, D, C on the instrument (starting on 1st space F-sharp)
20. Learn rote songs (sol-mi, sol-mi-do)
21. Reading F, E, D, and C (including singing)
22. Begin method book work
23. Long tones to build embouchure
24. B-flat (3rd space), left F (1st space)
25. Reading/sight-reading in the method book (add fingerings as needed)
26. Tetra chords
27. Octave key
28. Fork F, E-flat
29. Major scales
30. More reading and technical finger passages (adding fingerings as needed)

PRACTICAL TIPS

Assembly

♪ Always open the case on the floor.
♪ As with all woodwinds, take care not to put pressure or torque on the rods whenever possible.
  ◉ When necessary, press the keys themselves to get a better grip.
♪ Pay attention to bridge keys. Oboes may have as many as three (one between the bell and lower joint, two between the lower joint and upper joint).
♪ Always start from the bottom (bell) and work up the instrument.
♪ Don't forget to grease corks (and rub the grease in).
♪ Reeds are the last on and first off—don't risk accidental breakage.
♪ Cork grease must be rubbed into new corks. (You can tell by the color—light brown is less greased.)

Maintenance

- Sudden or dramatic temperature changes can cause the wood to split.
- Higher end instruments have more key work that can go out of adjustment—so buy good instruments but teach students to handle them carefully (and keep the nicest out of beginners' hands).
- Soak reeds in water.
    - Only the cane portion, never the cork.
    - Use a small cup, pill bottle, or other similarly shaped container.
    - Let reeds dry out after use.
    - Change the water often.
    - Avoid extreme temperatures of water.
- Never touch the tip of the reed with fingers.
- Always take off reed before moving around with the oboe.

Embouchure

- Significant backpressure requires strong facial muscles.
    - Face muscles take a significant time and repetition to develop. Be patient with beginning players.
    - Give students chances to rest.
    - Don't ask students to do things their faces aren't ready to support/handle.
- Avoid placing the entire reed in the mouth.
    - Some people suggest a little less than half the reed, while others suggest around 1/16 of an inch jutting into the mouth.
    - Reed position will influence timbre and intonation.
    - I usually start at about 50% of the vamp (shaved portion of the reed) and then adjust from there.
- Back teeth need to remain apart.
- Lips just barely cover the teeth/roll in.
- Teeth are even.
- Energy should be even around the lips—beginners like to bite to help overcome the backpressure.

- The reed needs room to vibrate, so firm but not biting.
- Watch for energized corners—beginners tend to be lax with corner energy that comes in towards the reed.
- Wind and face muscles have to work in conjunction with each other. You cannot build a strong oboe embouchure around bad wind.
- Controlling dynamics is partially a function of embouchure quality and strength. Take care not to overemphasize dynamics too soon.

Articulation

- Proper wind and embouchure are necessary for articulation; do not teach articulation until these are relatively well established.
- There are different schools of thought about where to touch the reed with the tongue:
  - All agree that the tongue should be relaxed underneath the reed and should come up to the reed to articulate.
  - Attacks should be quick and smooth.
  - Articulation is easier with proper wind support.
  - I teach tip to tip (tongue to reed) for beginners and then work to refine by sound.
- Keep the touch light.
- Keep the jaw still.
- Wind flows out when playing, in when breathing only. Articulation is more like waving a hand across an open faucet of water; the water never stops nor should the wind

Playing Position

- Hold the oboe at a 35°–45° angle
  - The angle is "straighter" than clarinet; if both instruments have the same playing position something has gone wrong with one of them.
- Head has to stay neutral—the oboe comes to the player, don't let student drop the head/chin to the instrument.
- Hold the oboe in the center of the body.
- Avoid resting the bell on the leg. It throws off head position/reed placement

Oboe

- Right thumb holds the weight.
  - Thumbnail towards the player, first knuckle under the thumb rest (similar to clarinet).
- Left thumb should be slightly offset from parallel (1–2 o'clock position) to reach the octave key(s).

Other Tips

- Force students to practice half-hole technique.
- Beginners need to practice using multiple fingerings for F.
  - This is so important I want to encourage directors *not* to think of one as primary and the other fingerings as alternative; instead, they are all primary.
- Closed tip openings (either due to the reed itself or due to biting) lead to pinched sounds.
- Squawky tones are mostly due to lack of a strong, correct embouchure and should fade over time.
  - Don't be in a hurry if the embouchure looks correct; building face muscles and control takes time.
- Only add vibrato after excellent, consistent embouchures are in place.
- Avoid the third octave until the embouchure is completely established.
- Don't start beginners on English horn.
- Practice finger patterns to give faces a break early in the year.
- Woodwind technique is largely making students do a large variety of technical patterns a ridiculous number of times.
- Force correct repetitions of difficult finger combinations:
  - Proper uses of all available F fingerings
  - To and from half-hole fingerings
  - Pinkies
- Over-soaking reeds can lead to warping and/or decreased lifespan.

TROUBLESHOOTING OBOE

Problem	Possible Causes	Possible Solutions
Small/Weak Tone	⊙ Lack of wind support ⊙ Biting/Embouchure too tight ⊙ Closed throat ⊙ Too little reed in mouth ⊙ Tight throat/tongue too high ⊙ Tip opening is reed is too small	⊙ Use more wind support ⊙ Decrease pressure with lower jaw or lower lip ⊙ Relax the throat as if saying "ooo" ⊙ Take more reed in mouth ⊙ Relax the throat/drop the lower tongue ⊙ Gently squeeze the sides of the reed; replace reed
Unfocused Tone	⊙ Poor reed ⊙ Improper wind direction ⊙ Reed is not centered in the mouth ⊙ Embouchure too loose overall ⊙ Reed angle is too extreme	⊙ Check reed for chipping/warping. Reed strength may be too hard/soft ⊙ When not adjusting specific note pitch, wind should be directed to the tip opening ⊙ Place reed in mouth properly/in the center ⊙ Energize the lips evenly around the reed ⊙ The reed should enter the mouth at an approximately 40°–45° angle
Weak, Fuzzy Tone	⊙ Reed too hard ⊙ Wind escaping through corners ⊙ Pad issues	⊙ Switch to a softer reed ⊙ Proper embouchure (solves poor embouchure formation) or more practice time outside of class (solves fatigue) ⊙ Leaking pads should be replaced, pads that are too open can be adjusted
Bright, Edgy, Reedy Tone	⊙ Reed too soft ⊙ Poorly cut reed ⊙ Too much reed in mouth ⊙ Overblowing	⊙ Switch to a harder reed ⊙ Replace reed ⊙ Take less reed in mouth ⊙ Control wind

Oboe

Loud, Spread Tone	⊙ Too much reed in mouth ⊙ Overblowing ⊙ Spread wind stream	⊙ Take less reed in mouth ⊙ Control the exhalation and keep the embouchure focused ⊙ Use proper embouchure to help focus wind to the tip opening
Poor High Note Response	⊙ Reed too soft ⊙ Biting/Embouchure too tight ⊙ Overblowing ⊙ Lack of wind support ⊙ Lack of embouchure support ⊙ Failure to use octave key(s)	⊙ Switch to harder reed ⊙ Relax embouchure ⊙ Control wind ⊙ Use more wind support ⊙ Energize the embouchure evenly around the reed ⊙ Use octave key(s) correctly
Poor Low Note Response	⊙ Reed too hard ⊙ Leaks ⊙ Lack of wind support ⊙ Biting/Embouchure too tight ⊙ Improper instrument angle	⊙ Switch to softer reed ⊙ Check instrument ⊙ Increase wind support or speed ⊙ Relax embouchure ⊙ The reed should enter the mouth at an approximately 40°–45° angle
Heavy Articulation	⊙ Too much tongue pressure on reed ⊙ Too much wind pressure behind tongue ⊙ Tongue touches too low on reed ⊙ Tongue is too high in the mouth and blocking wind stream	⊙ Use less tongue pressure/only use the tip tongue ⊙ Less intense wind pressure ⊙ Move the contact point higher on the reed ⊙ Lower the tongue placement

Flat Pitch	⊙ Lack of wind support	⊙ Increase/control wind
	⊙ Loose embouchure	⊙ Energize embouchure
	⊙ Wind stream angle too low	⊙ Raise wind stream angle
	⊙ Incorrect reed angle	⊙ The reed should enter the mouth at an approximately 40°–45° angle
	⊙ Too little reed in mouth	⊙ Take more reed
	⊙ Reed is too soft	⊙ Switch to harder reed
	⊙ Reed is too long	⊙ Replace reed with one that was made to be pushed in all the way
	⊙ Slouching	⊙ Sit with good posture
	⊙ Head/chin tilted down	⊙ Raise head/chin
	⊙ Lower jaw dropped	⊙ Raise lower jaw until embouchure pressure is consistent
Sharp Pitch	⊙ Too much reed in the mouth	⊙ Take less reed
	⊙ Biting	⊙ Relax embouchure
	⊙ Lack of wind support	⊙ Increase wind support
	⊙ Wind stream angle too high	⊙ Lower wind stream angel
	⊙ Incorrect reed angle	⊙ Adjust strap
	⊙ Reed is too hard	⊙ Switch to a softer reed
	⊙ Reed is too short	⊙ Replace reed with one that was made to be pushed in all the way

OBOE FINGERINGS

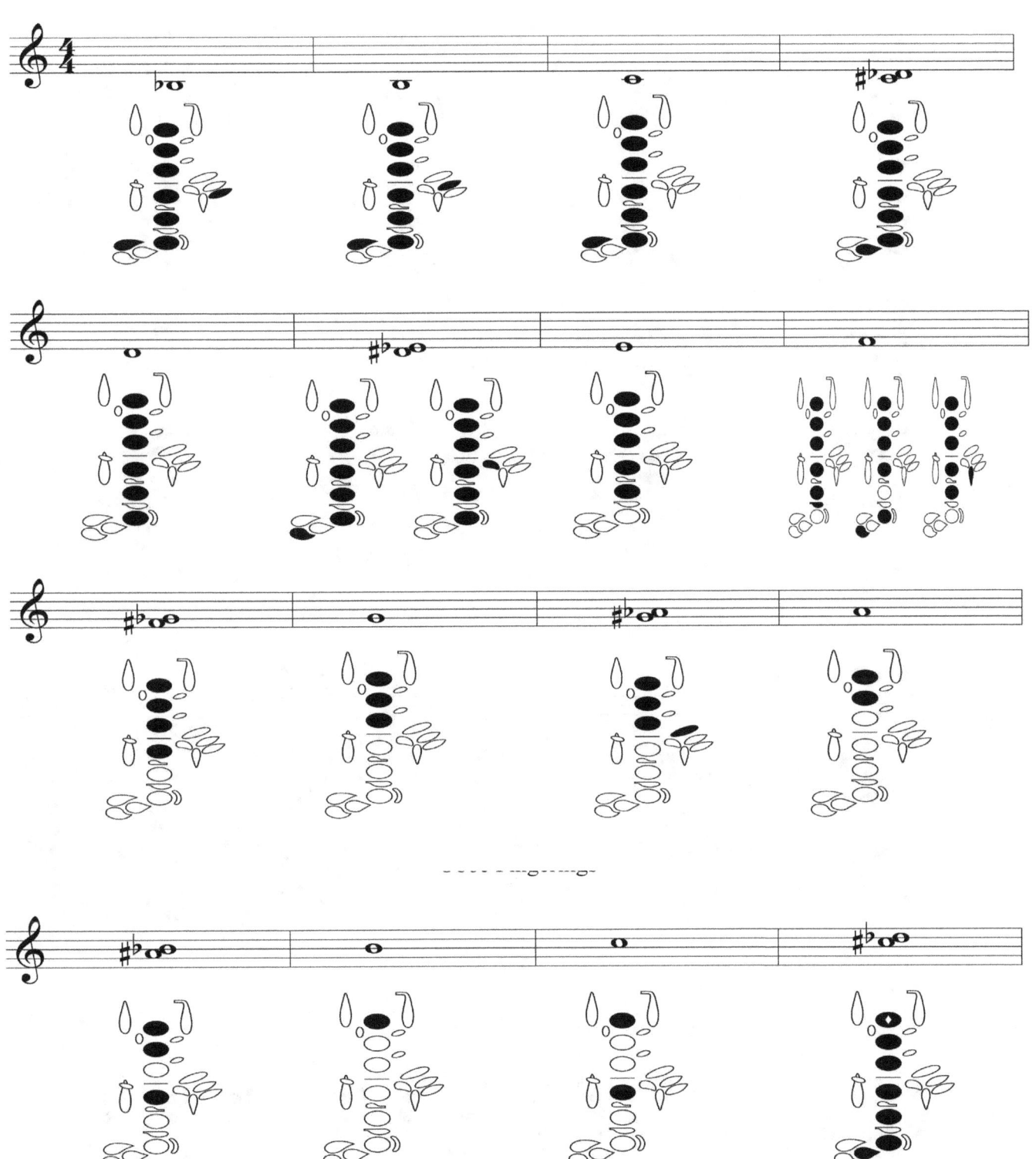

77

OBOE FINGERINGS

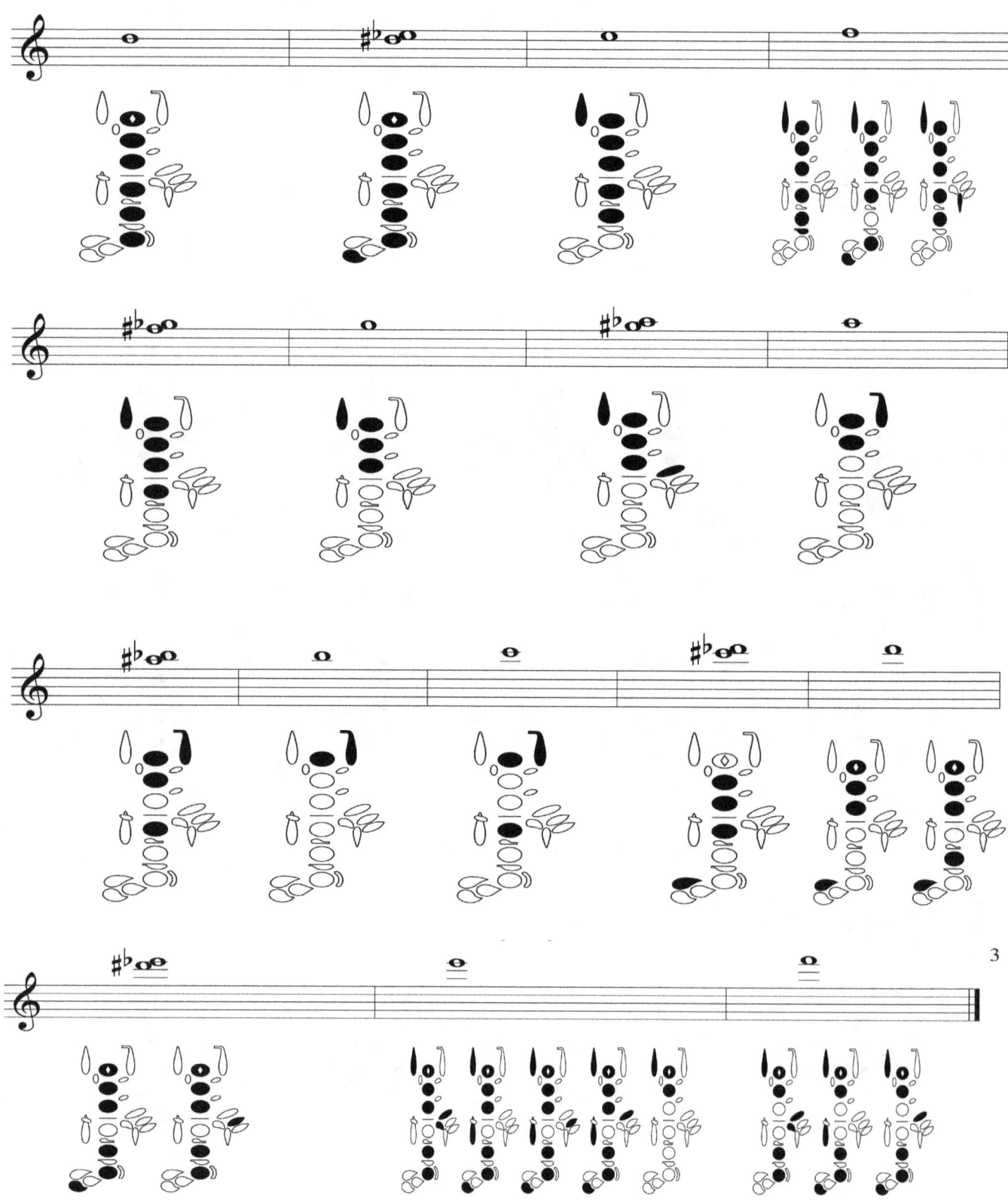

OBOE SUPPLEMENTAL EXERCISES

OBOE SUPPLEMENTAL EXERCISES

OBOE SUPPLEMENTAL EXERCISES

OBOE SUPPLEMENTAL EXERCISES

OBOE SUPPLEMENTAL EXERCISES

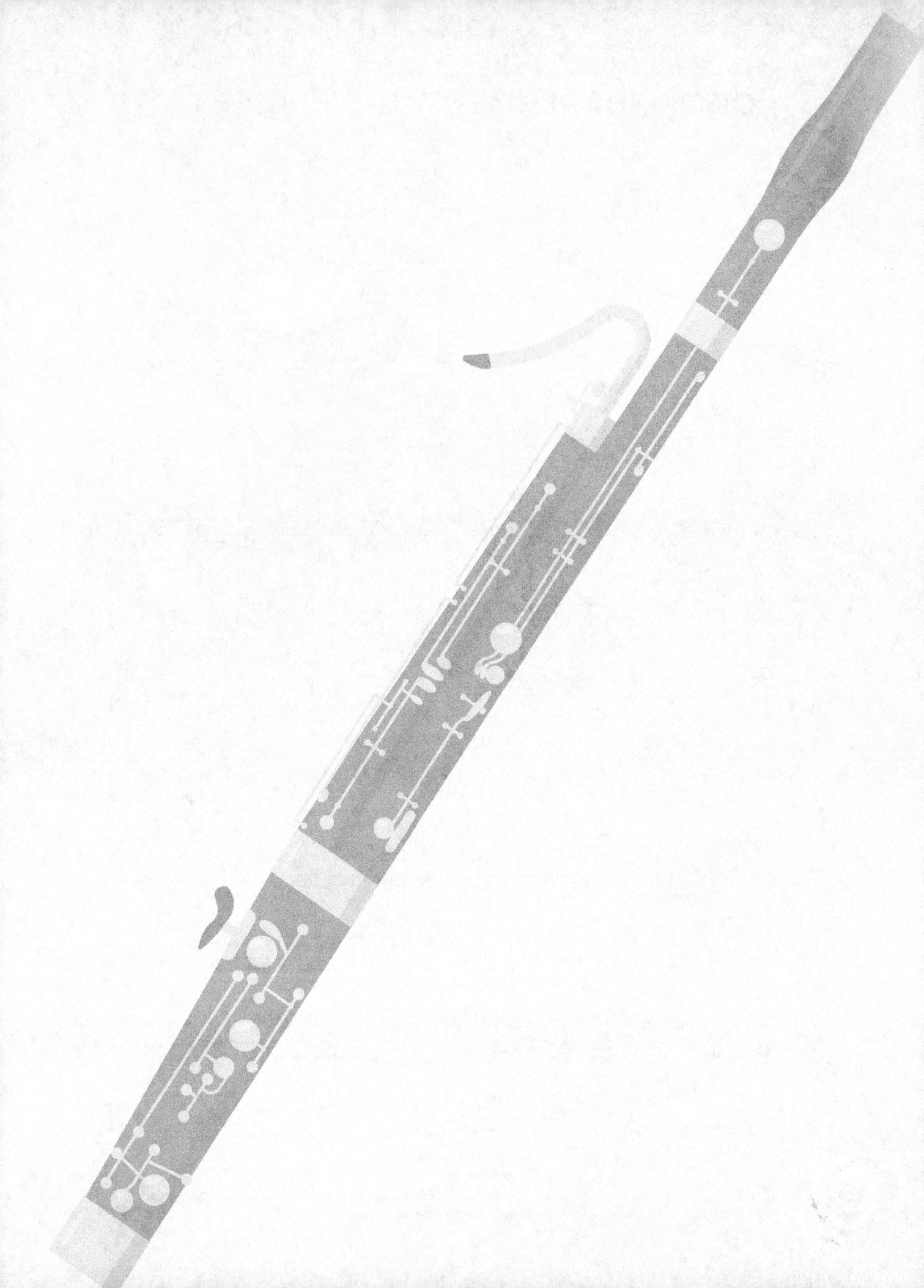

BASSOON

04

Bassoon

The origins of the bassoon are shrouded in mystery. The closest ancestors of the bassoon are the bass pommer/bombard (the largest shawm) or the dulcian, and these precursors were replaced by the bassoon beginning in the late 1600s. The bassoon has gone through considerable development over the years, and two separate models (German/Heckel and French/Buffet) have survived into modernity. Bassoons constructed with the French system have narrow bores, unique fingerings/key work, and relatively easier response in the upper register. While still used in Europe, French system bassoons are less common in the United States. German, or Heckel, bassoons, in contrast, have more keys and a larger bore than those of their French counterparts. The bassoon is a C instrument (non-transposing) and notation for bassoon is written in the sounding range (Figure B-1).

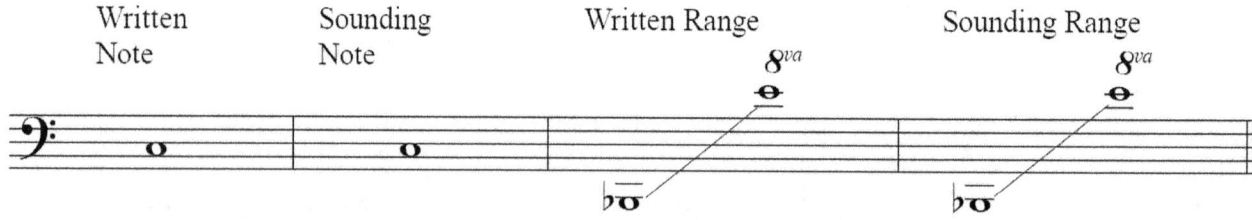

Figure B-1 Bassoon Ranges

While not rigid, below are approximate beginner, intermediate, and advanced ranges.

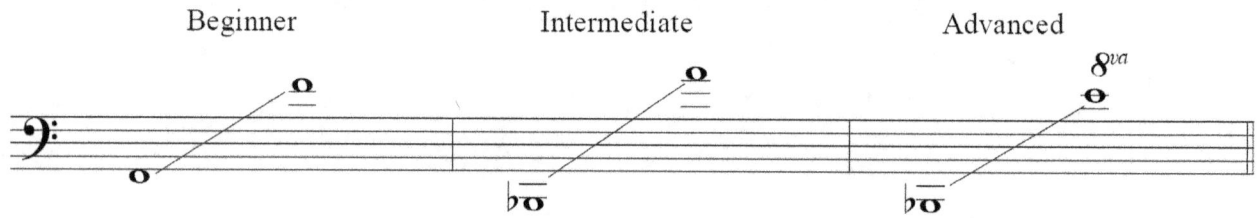

Figure B-2 Bassoon Skill Ranges

INSTRUMENT SELECTION

If bassoon is a beginner instrument in the program, student selection is an important task for the band director. Due to the nature of the instrument, students who have shown responsibility and the ability to follow directions are good fits for bassoon. Directors may measure this through individual experiences with the student or through references from other teachers. Prior musical training is also something to watch for, as the jump start regarding listening skills may be meaningful.

There are two physical considerations to keep in mind when selecting students for bassoon: fingers and underbite. The nature of bassoon fingerings requires the necessary reach both in terms of Fingers 1–6 and in regards to both thumbs. Students with either short fingers or that struggle with manual dexterity will find the beginning stages of bassoon performance frustrating. Have students hold an assembled instrument and help them to place their fingers in the correct places to assess finger length. Under bite, however, presents an egregious problem for future bassoonists. One of the most common approaches to embouchure requires a slight overbite, and students with an underbite may be required to put forth effort to make characteristic sounds on the instrument. Whenever possible, avoid placing students with underbites on bassoon.

EQUIPMENT

Double reeds are often school-owned instruments and selecting appropriate equipment can be daunting if you do not play bassoon. Below are some suggestions for future reference that may change due to model updates and manufacturer quality. Additionally, do not hesitate to ask other band directors or private instructors for their recommendations. Intermediate and professional bassoons are often made of wood, typically maple; however, reasonable quality resin bassoons exist. I recommend resin options for beginners due to their durability and consistency and wood options for more advanced players.

Obtaining quality reeds is the most important equipment consideration for bassoon. If possible, I would suggest starting with a private instructor or professional player in your area. If there are no bassoonists around to craft reeds for students, online options are available. Know that any online reeds will need adjustment to match both the player and instrument.

> **INSTRUMENT**
>
> Most Fox (Renard) models, specifically Renard Model 41 & 51 in resin or Renard Artist Model 220/ Renard Model 222 in maple

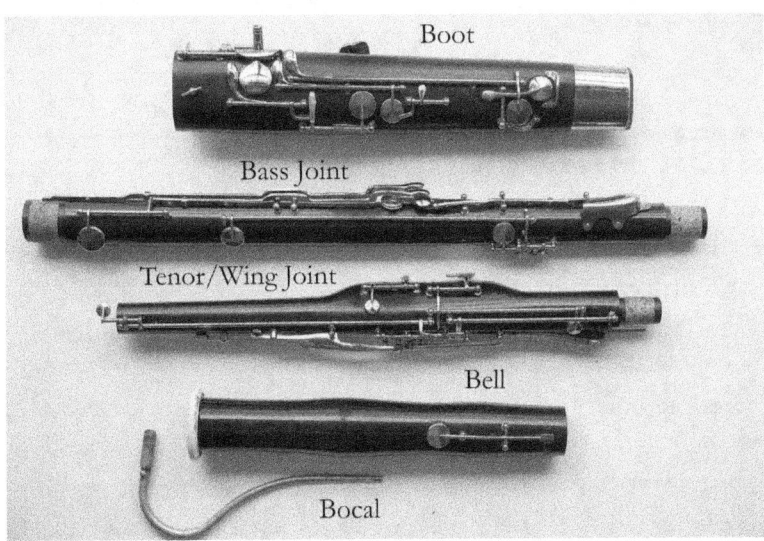

Figure B-3 Bassoon Parts

ASSEMBLY

Before putting the instrument together, be sure to address opening the case, naming the parts of the instrument, and handling reeds. If the instrument has corks instead of string, be sure to show students how to properly rub in cork grease. Additionally, point out the bridge keys to the students prior to their first attempt at putting the instrument together. Once students have a clear understanding of the parts and how to handle them, begin with inserting the tenor (wing) joint into the boot and aligning the bridge key. Next, insert the large end of the bass joint into the boot and secure the locking mechanism to the tenor joint. Then, press the key on the bell and insert the bell onto the bass joint, being careful to align the bridge key. Following bell placement, hook the boot to the seat strap before gently handling the bocal near the cork and inserting it into the top of the tenor/wing joint. Finally, place the reed on the end of the bocal by twisting with slight pressure (similarly to inserting a brass mouthpiece). The reed should either be parallel to the floor, or the right side should be slightly lower than the left.

There are multiple ways to assemble the bassoon, but whether you use the above approach or another the key takeaways are be aware of the bridge keys, put as little torque/pressure as possible on the keywork, handle bocals with care, always put reeds on last, and be sure the strap is properly secured.

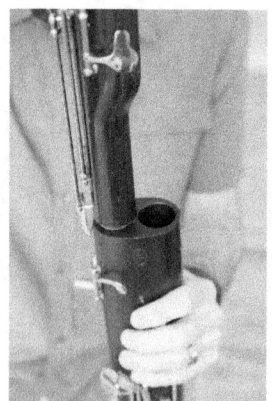

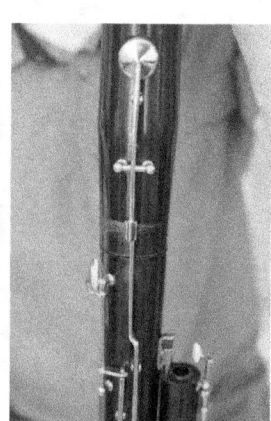
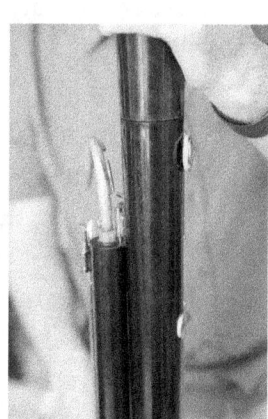

Figure B-4 Bassoon Assembly

TONE PRODUCTION AND EMBOUCHURE

After wind use, embouchure is the next core component of tone production, and in the case of the bassoon, the primary purpose of the embouchure is to facilitate proper reed vibration. To that end, embouchure cannot overcome a poor reed. Regularly check student reeds for quality (warping, chipping, etc.).

Bassoon reeds, like oboe reeds, have two blades that are cut to allow for vibration and held together, in the case of bassoon, by wires. Furthermore, the heart, as in single reeds, is the vertical center point of the reed that controls the basic vibration. With bassoon reeds, the heart may not be visible when held to the light, depending on the cut of the reed. This does not mean that the reed lacks a heart; rather evaluating

Bassoon

the heart is more complicated depending on the manner in which the reed was created. Reeds need to be soaked in fresh water, ideally at room temperature. While there are different schools of thought about if the entire bassoon reed should be soaked or just the part prior to the binding, note that the reed must be wet, and the two blades must seal at the corners in order to produce a quality tone. Generally, reeds only need to be soaked for a few minutes—although there are exceptions.

The core bassoon embouchure is relatively simple to form and teach. Students should open their jaw and bring their lower jaw back slightly (unless they have a natural overbite). At the same time, students can bring their lips somewhat over their teeth and push the corners of their mouths toward the center, as in a whistle. Finally, students should place the reed in the center of the mouth so that the upper lip nearly touches the first wire (but does not actually make contact) and then seal their lips around the reed. As we discussed earlier, reeds must be tuned to (often to A = 440) on each particular instrument and bassoon reeds that are relatively in tune will crow between E-flat and F.

Extreme registers will require students to make embouchure adjustments, with high notes generally requiring greater energy/firmer embouchure and low notes requiring a more relaxed/soft embouchure. Furthermore, the jaw should be dropped and the overbite increased for the extremely low register. Like all reed instruments, these adjustments should be made without biting the reed with the teeth.

 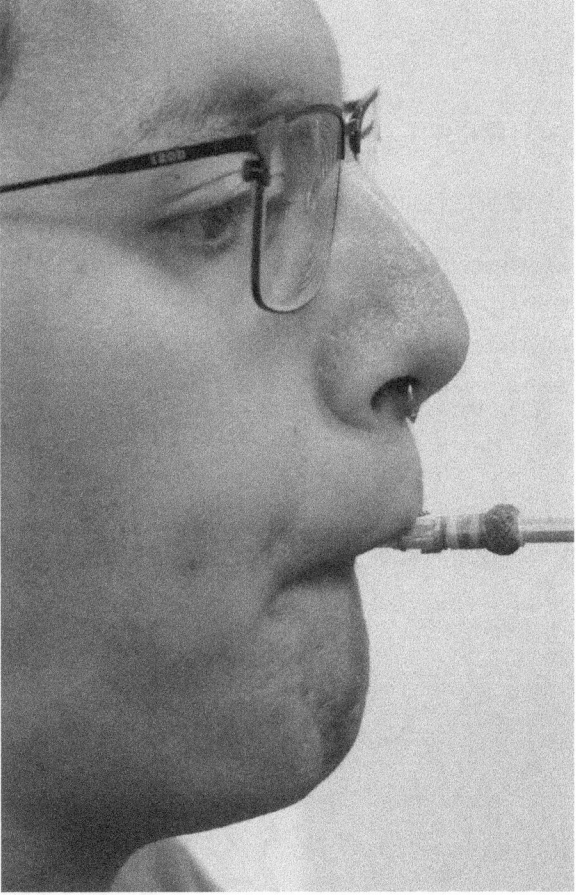

Figure B-5 Bassoon Embouchure Figure B-5 Bassoon Embouchure

Bassoon

EMBOUCHURE LESSON PLAN/INSTRUCTIONAL SEQUENCE

Subject: Bassoon   **Grade:** 6   **Date:**

♪ **Concept:**
Making a characteristic tone on the reed

♪ **Behavioral Learning Objective:**
Students will be able to form a characteristic embouchure and assess themselves or others regarding embouchure.

♪ **Standards:**
MU:Pr5.3.E.5a/MU:Pr6.1.E.5a (National Standards example) or TEKS 117.208.C.3.B (State Standards example)

 **Vocabulary:** Embouchure, energize, lips, teeth

 **Materials:** Reed

 **Time:** 10–15 minutes

Procedures

1. Students point their index finger at their mouth.

2. **Method 1:** Students open the jaw and bring it slightly back from the natural resting position (unless they have a natural overbite, then they simply drop the jaw).
   Method 2: Students open the jaw and keep teeth aligned.

3. Students bring the corners of their mouth towards the center (as in saying "ooo") and slightly roll their lips over their teeth.

4. Students place their index finger in the center of their mouth so that their upper lip nearly touches the first knuckle and seal their lips around their finger (avoid biting).

ASSESSMENT
Evaluate embouchure by comparing to an ideal image of bassoon embouchure, check sounding pitch with a tuning (F is generally ideal—double crows are allowed).

Bassoon

ARTICULATION

Like all wind instruments, proper wind support is necessary for correct articulation. Only the tip of the tongue is used to articulate, and the tongue acts as a release valve for the wind at the start of a note. Students should keep the tongue relaxed and loose and the top of the tip of the tongue should touch the tip of the center of the *bottom blade*. Take care to remind students not to close up the opening between the blades with their tongue, which is commonly caused by using the very edge of the tongue instead of the top surface to articulate. This may lead to consistently heavy or distorted attacks. Furthermore, tonguing directly on the opening makes fast articulation nearly impossible.

Some students may struggle with using the middle of their tongue to articulate, which generates a muddy, forceful attack. This problem is often exacerbated by reed placement, so directors should always check to see if the student has taken too much or too little reed in their mouth as part of diagnosing tongue placement issues. If the reed in the correct place, students may need to adjust their tongue placement inside the oral cavity. Have students experiment with arching their tongue slightly to allow the tip to come up to the reed.

ARTICULATION LESSON PLAN

Subject: Bassoon   **Grade:** 6   **Date:**

- ♪ **Concept:**
  Articulating correctly on a variety of rhythms

- ♪ **Behavioral Learning Objective:**
  Students will be able to perform articulated notes in a variety of rhythms while maintaining proper embouchure.

- ♪ **Standards:**
  MU:Pr5.3.E.5a/MU:Pr6.1.E.5a/ MU:Pr4.2.E.5a (National Standards example) or TEKS 117.208.C.3.B (State Standards example)

Vocabulary:
Articulation, tonguing, quarter notes, stability, legato

Materials:
Mouthpiece, neck, reed, ligature, white/chalk board, entire instrument (optional)

Time:
15–20 minutes

Bassoon

Procedures

1. Students crow on the reed to review embouchure and wind use.
2. Students touch top of the tip of the tongue to the bottom of the tip of the reed.
3. Optional: Teacher models articulation sound for students.
4. Students blow wind and move their tongue without the reed—teacher assesses wind consistency.
5. Teacher models unmetered articulation for students.
6. Students blow wind and move their tongue with proper embouchure on reed—unmetered practice
7. Teacher models metered quarter notes—full value.
8. Students perform quarter notes on reed. (Be sure to watch/listen for students who are cheating by using a breath or "who" start.)
9. Optional: Students articulate notes on the entire instrument.

ASSESSMENT

Assess students for connected/legato articulation and correct rhythmic performance by listening to individuals and the group.

PLAYING POSITION

Similar to the saxophone, the bassoon uses support equipment to help the player hold the instrument. There are two separate playing positions for the bassoon; however, these are dependent on the support equipment used. Beginning band students most often use the seat strap, even though it does not allow for playing from a standing position. This is largely due to the weight of the bassoon, which can be difficult for younger students to manage (the same reason it is wise to avoid assigning a bari sax to a beginner). When using a seat strap, directors should be aware that it may create a weight imbalance on the students' left side in order to balance the instrument. Additionally, incorrect seat strap placement commonly leads to poor posture; therefore students should adjust their seat strap so that the reed/bocal enters the mouth at a flat angle/parallel to the lips and the bassoon itself should make approximately 50°–55° angle with the ground/chair (see Figures B-5 and B-6).

Bassoon

The neck strap allows students to play standing up and provides better balance overall. Many professionals view the use of the crutch/hand rest as essential when using a neck strap to provide an anchor point on the right hand without increasing tension, whereas there is no consensus on crutch use in combination with the seat strap. One final note about instrument position: the bassoon will cross the student's body so that the *bell is to the left side of the player's head* (Figure B-6). Playing positions should be as free from tension as possible; therefore try to strike a balance between reed angle, balancing the instrument, and keeping the fingers free of tension.

As with all woodwinds, the left hand is closer to the mouth with the Left Thumb perpendicular to the bassoon and relaxed across the thumb keys. The fingers curve around to the tone holes in a natural "C" and the instrument itself should be balanced by the base of Finger 1 (similar to flute, although the angle is different). Parallel to the clarinet, student should use the pads of their fingers to cover the tone holes, not the tips. The Left Pinky should gently rest on the D-sharp key.

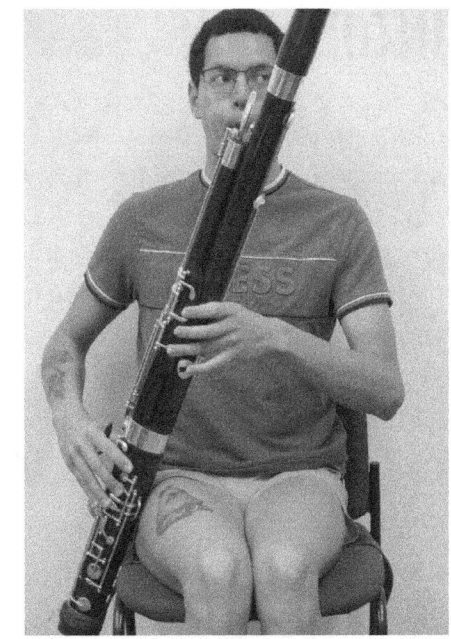

Figure B-6 Bassoon Playing Position

Fingers 4 and 5 will cover the tone holes, while Finger 6 will skip the next available key and instead rest on the G key (Figure B-7). If using a crutch, be sure to adjust it for comfort and student finger length. Finally, the Right Thumb should hover about the E key (commonly referred to as either the pan or pancake key due to its shape).

   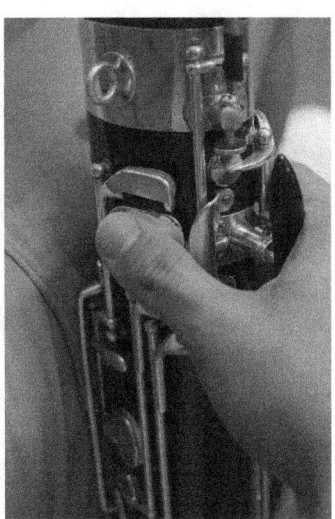

Figure B-7 Bassoon Hand Position

INTONATION

Like with oboe, the bassoon lacks a mechanical approach to large-scale intonation adjustment. Still, some band directors may try to adjust tuning through bocal placement in the tenor/wing joint. The nature of the whisper key pad, however, makes this a limited option as the pad must align with the vent and seal properly for the instrument to work as intended. Instead, the primary mechanical consideration for intonation with the bassoon is actually the reed itself. I strongly suggest you reach out to a bassoon private instructor to help you with making reed adjustments, as there are many ways to destroy a double reed through ignorance and the lack of appropriate tools. Furthermore, there are some great resources online and in book form if you really want to take up the art of reed making, and Westphall (1993) has a fantastic introduction to the sometimes-maddening task of managing reeds.

In a pinch you can use needle-nosed pliers to adjust the wires on a bassoon reed, which in turn will alter the tip opening between the blades. By adjusting the wires from the sides of the reed, you can increase the tip opening, thus lowering the reed pitch. Conversely, by adjusting the wires from the top/bottom of the reed you can close the tip opening and raise the reed pitch. Such adjustments may have the added benefit of adjusting the ease of producing a crow on the reed for beginners; however, they should be used with caution. Adjusting the wires can sacrifice tone quality, responsiveness, and actually end up shortening the lifespan of the reed. Quality bassoon reeds will typically have an upper crow somewhere between E and F-sharp. Like with the oboe, this is an important aspect of creating reeds, but more of a rule of thumb for directors.

After eliminating reed quality as a source of intonation concerns, directors can move on to bocal length. As is the case with all wind instruments (thanks, physics!), the longer the vibrating wind column the lower the sound. Therefore, if a student consistently plays sharp on a good reed, then a longer bocal would lower the pitch. Bocals are typically numbered from 00 to 4, where higher numbers mean longer bocal length and lower pitch. Letters, on the other hand, address timbral aspects of the bocal, such as the material used, bocal shape, and bocal wall thickness. It is worth noting that both length number and timbral letter markings are not standardized across manufacturers, so I suggest buying bocals from the same company that made the bassoon.

The bassoon can be tuned using the following notes (Figure B-8):

Figure B-8 Bassoon Tuning Notes

Bassoon

Additionally, the following notes some of the more egregious notes on the bassoon in terms of intonation (Figure B-9):

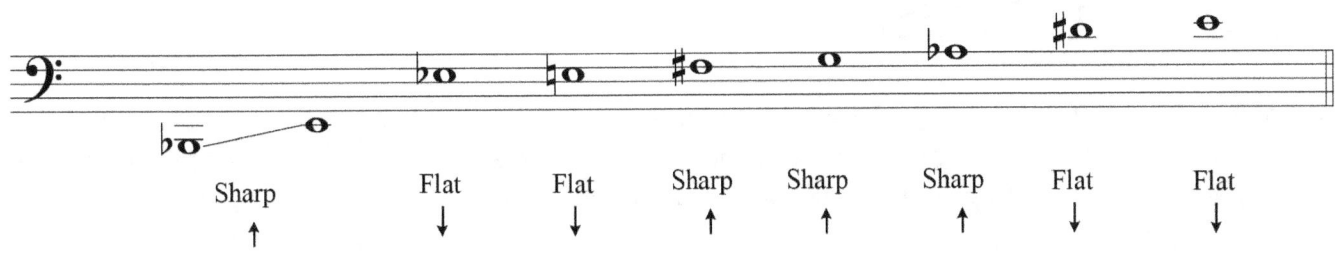

Figure B-9 Bassoon Intonation Challenges

Once students are playing on appropriate reeds and bocals, intonation adjustments largely rely on the embouchure, wind, and alternate fingerings. Typically, firmer embouchures result in sharper pitch, while looser embouchures play flat. Furthermore, taking more reed in the mouth will raise the pitch and taking less reed will lower the pitch, just like on oboe. Reed placement will also impact tone quality, so I suggest being cautious when asking players to adjust pitch this way to avoid sacrificing timbre for intonation. Similarly, wind that is aimed upward will raise the pitch and wind that is focused downward lowers the pitch. These embouchure/wind adjustments are best when the intonation only requires slight adjustments. Using alternate fingerings can drastically change the pitch, but also drastically change tone quality. Changing fingerings may also be impractical depending on the technical demands of the music, and the use of alternate fingerings should be weighed against tone and technique considerations.

VIBRATO

Bassoonists generally use diaphragmatic vibrato, however there are rare examples of jaw vibrato usage among bassoonists. While the field as a whole uses the term "diaphragmatic," this type of vibrato used by bassoonists and flutists involves the wind column from the lungs into the oral cavity. I use wind pulses on the hand or with a piece of paper to give students a tactile or visual example of how the energized wind column can create vibrato. For instance, I ask my students to hold their hand in front of their mouth and blow pulses without inhaling or allowing the wind to stop completely. Some students may try to move their jaw or mouth; however, they will be unable to produce consistent pulses (which I model for the students who are struggling). The paper activity is similar, in that students hold a sheet of paper in front of their mouths and blow pulses to move the paper. The goal is that the paper should move back and forth distinctly without ever coming completely to rest. Both approaches stress the importance of *slight* variations of wind intensity.

Once on the instrument, students should initially practice vibrato isolated from other techniques. Midrange notes on the bassoon provide the best place to practice vibrato, due in part to the ease in tone production of notes in the middle of the instrument. As I mentioned in the previous chapter, I strongly advocate for introducing vibrato unmetered to allow for students to develop physical control without developing a habit of rigidity.

SPECIAL TECHNIQUES

The bassoon has two common techniques that are essential for beginners to learn as part of their initial time with the instrument: half-hole and flicking/venting. Half-hole is the shorthand for the need to partially vent the tone hole for Finger 1 to produce notes an octave higher than the closed fingering on certain pitches (F-sharp, G, and A-flat). To do this, bassoonists must finger the lower fingering for the desired note while rolling Finger 1 partially off the tone hole. This is made more complicated by the fact that the optimum venting for each note varies slightly, with the F-sharp requiring the largest half-hole aperture and the A-flat requiring a half-hole aperture that is quite small. Also, students should press the whisper key whenever half-hole fingerings are used.

Flicking/venting involves the quick press/release of keys to increase the responsiveness of certain notes (fourth line A to D/E-flat above the staff), particularly when slurring. The keys involved in flicking/venting are on the tenor (wing) joint above the whisper key and are operated by the LT. Students should use flicking/venting when the music contains a leap from a note in the lower register to one of the notes in the flicking/venting range mentioned above. As their fingers change to the fingering for the new note, the Left Thumb rapidly presses and releases the appropriate flick/vent key. This motion should be in-sync with the rest of the fingers, like with any fingering change. Flicking/venting is especially important when leaps are accompanied by slurs, as the response issues common to the particular notes become considerably more glaring. Dietz (1998) laid out an excellent breakdown of flicking exercises for use with young bassoonists in his book *Teaching Woodwinds: A Method and Resource Handbook for Music Educators*.

IDEAL AURAL IMAGES

1. Albrecht Holder	2. Milan Turkovic	3. Gustavo Núñez
4. Krysten Wolfe Jenson	5. Judith LeClair	6. Julie Price
7. David McGill	8. Richard Ranti	9. George Sakakeeny

Bassoon

SELECTED BEGINNER REPERTOIRE

Bocal Majority's Beginner Boot Camp Books (my favorite) – by Bohls and Auerbach, published Bocal Majority Woodwinds

Rubank Elementary Method for Bassoon – by Skornicka, published by Hal Leonard

Learn to Play Bassoon, Bk 1: A Carefully Graded Method That Develops Well-Rounded Musicianship – by Eisenhauer, published by Alfred

BEGINNER BASSOON SEQUENCE EXAMPLE

The sequence listed below is merely a suggestion and is not meant to be exhaustive or perfect. Instead, this sequence should serve as a leaping-off point for directors to plan their own beginner courses. Also, keep in mind that many of the items, particularly at the beginning, will happen concurrently. This is partly because students will not have the physical or mental endurance to spend an entire class on one topic or content item. Furthermore, beginning instruction can be summed up in the phrase, "Teach, reteach, and then teach it again." Rarely will there be a class of beginners that understand and can correctly play an instrument the first time, so plan to review everything you introduce.

1. Breathing
2. Posture
3. Opening the case/parts of the instrument/care of the instrument
4. Embouchure (using thumb)
5. Proper hand position/how to hold the instrument
6. Embouchure round 2 (on reed)/first sounds
7. Finger exercises
8. Introduce note symbols (rhythmic)
9. Long tones on reed
10. Note shapes/releases
11. Counting quarter note rhythms
12. Articulation (unmetered and metered)
13. Reed to full instrument sounds
14. F, E, D, and C on the instrument (starting on 4th line F)
15. Embouchure round 3 (reed checking crow pitch around E-flat)
16. Learn rote songs (mi-re-do)
17. Counting quarter/half/whole note rhythms
18. The staff and reading F, E, D, and C (include singing)
19. B, B-flat, A, G, and F on the instrument (starting with 2nd line B)
20. Learn rote songs (sol-mi, sol-mi-do)
21. Reading B, B-flat, A, G, and F (including singing)
22. Begin method book work
23. Long tones to build embouchure
24. E-flat (3rd space) and G (4th space)

25. Reading/sight-reading in the method book (add fingerings as needed)
26. Tetra chords
27. Flicking (F-sharp, G, and A)
28. Major scales
29. More reading and technical finger passages

PRACTICAL TIPS

Assembly

- Always open the case on the floor.
- Only handle the bocal near the cork. Never put it in the wing joint while holding the small end.
- Be aware of the bridge keys.
    - Both careful handling and careful alignment are necessary.
- Reeds are always the last thing on and the first thing off.
- Bassoons can be assembled multiple ways (not just using the sequence I've given above).
- Only corks need cork grease, string (often red) does not.

Embouchure

- Even energy around the reed is important, missing or significantly uneven teeth can lead to challenges.
    - Bottom lip provides support without cutting off reed vibration.
    - Avoid bunching the chin as it can also lead to uneven support for the blades.
- Poor embouchures lead to intonation problems.
    - Too loose plays flat.
    - Too tight plays sharp.
- Depending on the embouchure taught, underbites may not be a good fit for the bassoon.

Articulation

- ♪ Proper wind and embouchure are necessary for articulation; do not teach articulation until these are relatively well established.
- ♪ Wind flows out when playing, in when breathing only. Articulation is more like waving a hand across an open faucet of water—the water never stops nor should the wind.
- ♪ While there are differences of opinion about specific placement, most agree that students shouldn't touch the top blade when articulating.

Playing Position

- ♪ This instrument always comes to the player, not the other way around.
  - ◉ Students sometimes get lazy with their strap positions—be vigilant about posture.
- ♪ Reeds should not point down towards the ground/enter the mouth at a downward angle.
- ♪ Generally, the bell should cross to the player's left side.

Other Tips

- ♪ Woodwind technique is largely making students do a large variety of technical patterns a ridiculous number of times.
- ♪ Intonation is complicated.
  - ◉ Consistent tone is a prerequisite for effective intonation.
  - ◉ Reeds matter with intonation more than directors imagine.
  - ◉ So does everything else (embouchure, tongue position, wind support, pad opening height, etc.).
  - ◉ Bassoon bocal lengths are a special consideration and greatly impact intonation in the middle and upper registers.
    - Westphal[13] suggested that flat E-naturals and Fs combined with either sharp middle G or fork E-flat is a reasonable indication of bocal length problems.
    - Bocals of the same length/number can still sound different with different players—partially due to the material, variances in the manufacturing process, and/or match with the player and reed.
- ♪ Force correct repetitions of difficult finger combinations:
  - ◉ Flicking
  - ◉ To and from half-hole fingerings
  - ◉ Fingerings that require lesser used thumb keys (not whisper key)

---

13   Westphal, 1990, 222.

Bassoon

- String (usually red) doesn't need cork grease.
- Oversoaking reeds can lead to warping and/or decreased lifespan.
- Reed placement will impact tone and tuning.
  - Lips should not touch the first wire.

TROUBLESHOOTING BASSOON

Problem	Possible Causes	Possible Solutions
Small/Weak Tone	<ul><li>Lack of wind support</li><li>Biting/embouchure too tight</li><li>Too little reed in mouth</li><li>Tight throat/tongue too high</li><li>Tip opening is reed is too small</li></ul>	<ul><li>Use more wind support</li><li>Decrease pressure with lower jaw or lower lip</li><li>Take more reed in mouth</li><li>Relax the throat/drop the lower tongue</li><li>Adjust reed wires to open the tip; replace reed</li></ul>
Unfocused Tone	<ul><li>Poor reed</li><li>Improper wind direction</li><li>Reed is not centered in the mouth</li><li>Embouchure too loose overall</li><li>Reed angle is too extreme</li></ul>	<ul><li>Check reed for chipping/warping; reed strength may be too hard/soft</li><li>When not adjusting specific note pitch, wind should be directed to the tip opening</li><li>Place reed in mouth properly/in the center</li><li>Energize the lips evenly around the reed</li><li>The reed should enter the mouth mostly straight</li></ul>
Weak, Fuzzy Tone	<ul><li>Reed too hard</li><li>Wind escaping through corners</li><li>Pad issues</li></ul>	<ul><li>Switch to a softer reed</li><li>Proper embouchure (solves poor embouchure formation) or more practice time outside of class (solves fatigue)</li><li>Leaking pads should be replaced, pads that are too open can be adjusted</li></ul>

Bassoon

Bright, Edgy, Reedy Tone	⊙ Reed too soft ⊙ Poorly cut reed ⊙ Tension in embouchure ⊙ Overblowing ⊙ Too much reed in mouth	⊙ Switch to a harder reed ⊙ Replace reed ⊙ Relax embouchure ⊙ Control wind ⊙ Take less reed
Loud, Spread Tone	⊙ Too much reed in mouth ⊙ Overblowing ⊙ Spread wind stream	⊙ Take less reed in mouth ⊙ Control the exhalation and keep the embouchure focused ⊙ Use proper embouchure to help focus wind to the tip opening
Lack of Dynamic Control	⊙ Wind control and direction inconsistent ⊙ Extreme changes in timbre/intonation ⊙ Seemingly random dynamic control issues	⊙ Practice long tones at varying dynamic levels ⊙ Keep embouchure consistent across dynamic levels ⊙ Use proper reed strength
Poor High Note Response	⊙ Reed too soft ⊙ Biting/embouchure too tight ⊙ Overblowing ⊙ Lack of wind support ⊙ Lack of embouchure support	⊙ Switch to harder reed ⊙ Relax embouchure ⊙ Control wind ⊙ Use more wind support ⊙ Energize the embouchure evenly around the reed
Poor Low Note Response	⊙ Reed too hard ⊙ Leaks ⊙ Lack of wind support ⊙ Biting/embouchure too tight	⊙ Switch to softer reed ⊙ Check instrument ⊙ Increase wind support or speed ⊙ Relax embouchure
Slurs are choppy or disconnected	⊙ Wind stream changes unnecessarily for smaller slurs ⊙ Embouchure not set ⊙ Fingers are uncoordinated ⊙ Not flicking when appropriate	⊙ Maintain steady wind stream ⊙ Keep the embouchure steady ⊙ Fingers should be close to the keys and move in unison ⊙ Use flicking

Heavy Articulation	⊙ Too much tongue pressure on reed	⊙ Use less tongue pressure/only use the tip tongue
	⊙ Too much wind pressure behind tongue	⊙ Less intense wind pressure
	⊙ Tongue touches too low on reed	⊙ Move the contact point higher on the reed
	⊙ Tongue is too high in the mouth and blocking wind stream	⊙ Lower the tongue placement
Flat Pitch	⊙ Too little reed in mouth	⊙ Take more reed
	⊙ Bocal is too long	⊙ Choose a shorter bocal
	⊙ Loose embouchure	⊙ Energize embouchure
	⊙ Lack of wind support	⊙ Control wind
	⊙ Wind stream angle too low	⊙ Raise wind stream angle
	⊙ Incorrect reed angle	⊙ Adjust strap
	⊙ Reed is too soft	⊙ Switch to harder reed
	⊙ Reed is too long	⊙ Replace reed with one that was made to be pushed in all the way
Sharp Pitch	⊙ Too much reed in the mouth	⊙ Take less reed
	⊙ Bocal is too short	⊙ Chose a longer bocal
	⊙ Biting	⊙ Relax embouchure
	⊙ Lack of wind support	⊙ Increase wind support
	⊙ Wind stream angle too high	⊙ Lower wind stream angel
	⊙ Incorrect reed angle	⊙ Adjust strap
	⊙ Reed is too hard	⊙ Switch to a softer reed
	⊙ Reed is too short	⊙ Replace reed with one that was made to be pushed in all the way

BEGINNER BASSOON FINGERINGS

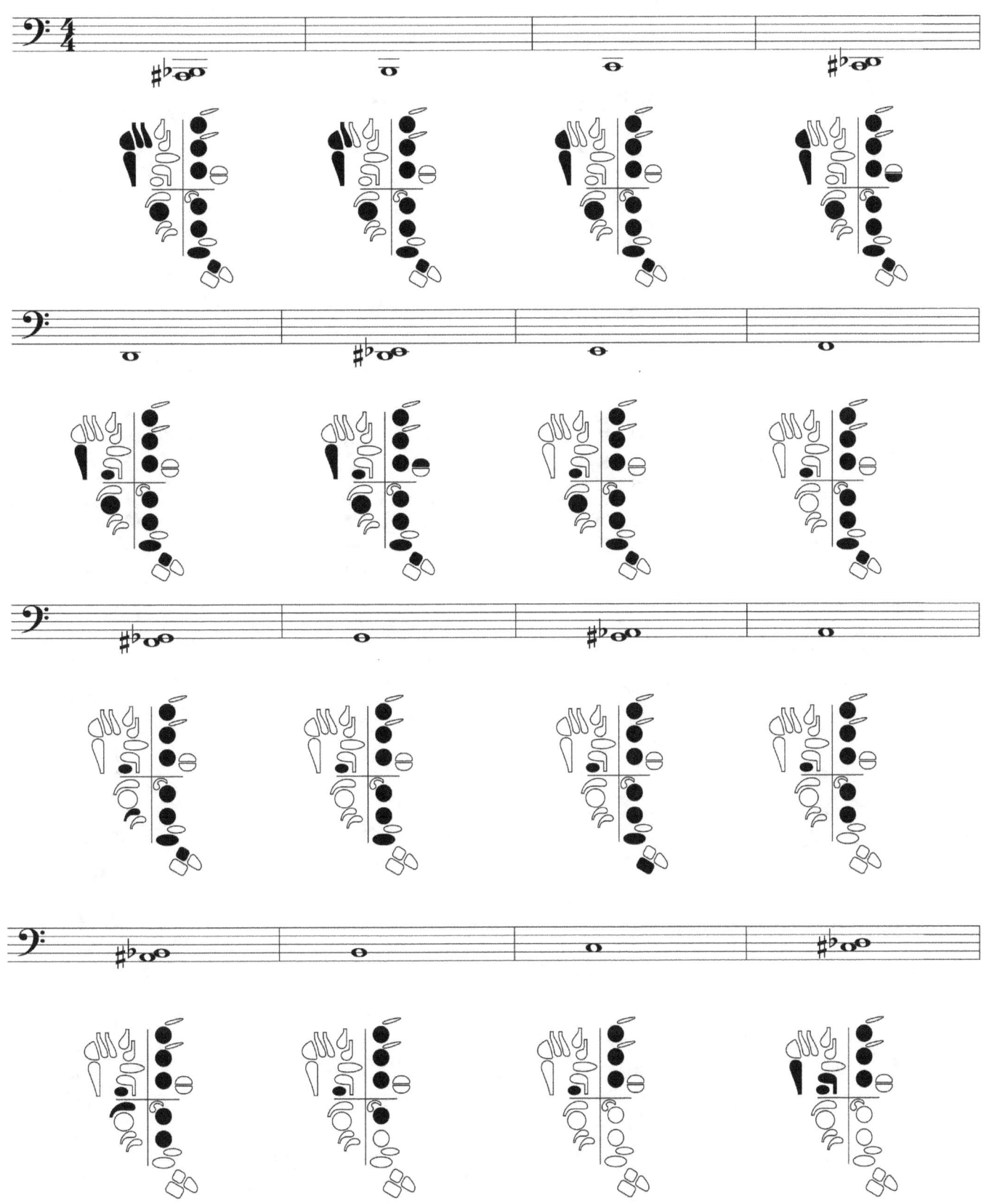

BEGINNER BASSOON FINGERINGS

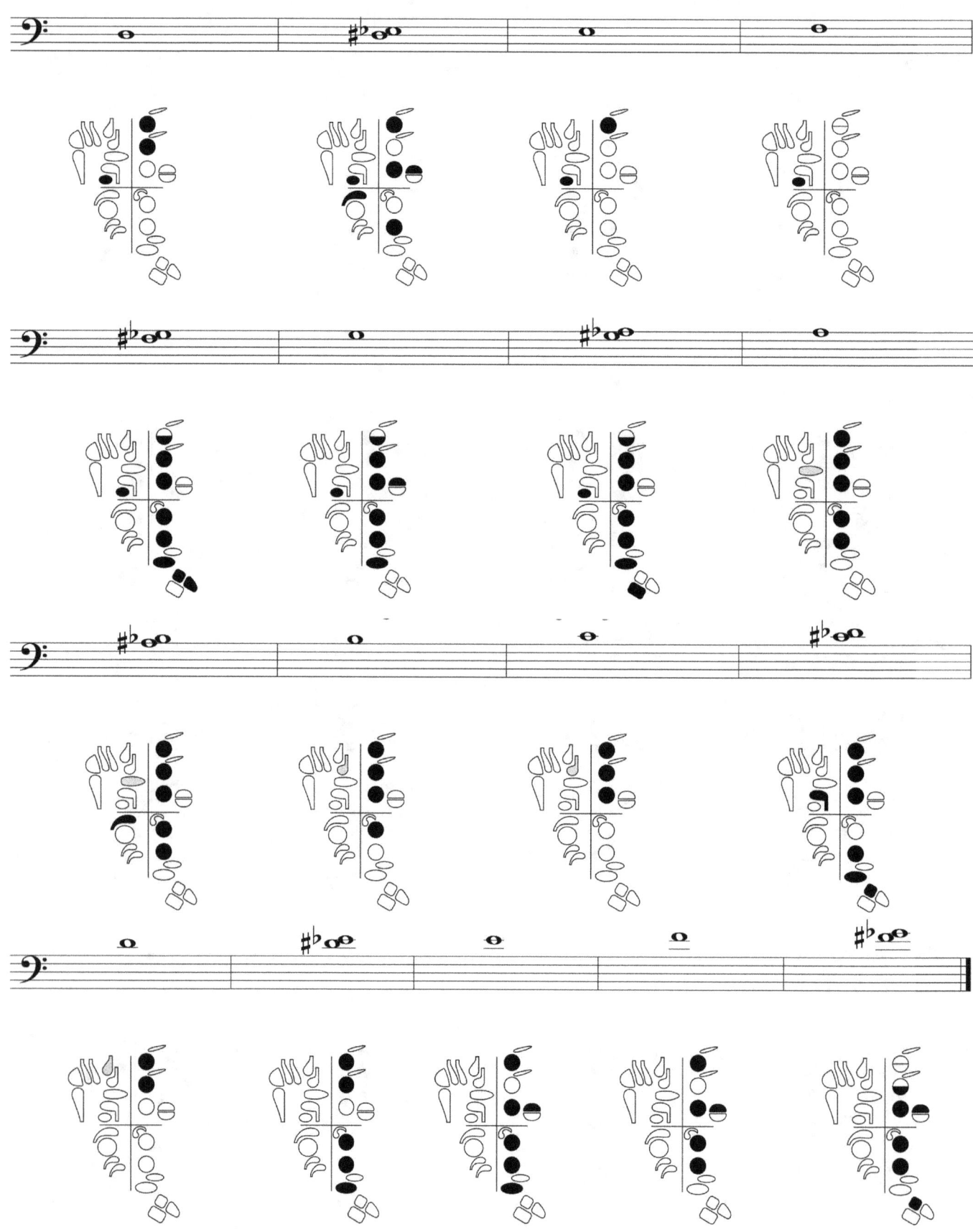

BASSOON SUPPLEMENTAL EXERCISES

BASSOON SUPPLEMENTAL EXERCISES

© 2025 Agogic Pres

Agogic Press grants permission to duplicate this worksheet for non-profit, educational use only, provided each copy includes this copyright notice.
Copies may not be sold or included in any materials offered for sale or for any form of profit.

BASSOON SUPPLEMENTAL EXERCISES

BASSOON SUPPLEMENTAL EXERCISES

© 2025 Agogic Press

Agogic Press grants permission to duplicate this worksheet for non-profit, educational use only, provided each copy includes this copyright notice.
Copies may not be sold or included in any materials offered for sale or for any form of profit.

BASSOON SUPPLEMENTAL EXERCISES

BASSOON SUPPLEMENTAL EXERCISES

BASSOON SUPPLEMENTAL EXERCISES

SINGLE REEDS

The single reeds (clarinet and saxophone) share many commonalities, and yet retain significant differences. All single reeds produce sound through the vibration of a reed anchored to a mouthpiece via assorted styles of ligatures. Before discussing the specific quirks of clarinet and saxophone, it is necessary to have an understanding of the foundational aspects of single reed sound production.

In order to evaluate reeds, it is necessary to understand the parts of the single reed. The bottom of the reed is referred to as the heel. Immediately above the heel is the stock, which has an unshaved cane appearance. The vamp is the part of the reed where bark has been removed to allow for vibration. The vamp contains the heart of the reed (which is the vertical center point of the reed that controls basic vibration), the shoulders (which are on either side of the heart), and the tip (which is the thinnest portion of the reed). See Figure SR-1 for a visual representation of the single reed.

Good reeds are those that play and respond well across the full range of the instrument and the full range of dynamics, respond well to articulations, and give the appropriate amount of wind resistance. Bad

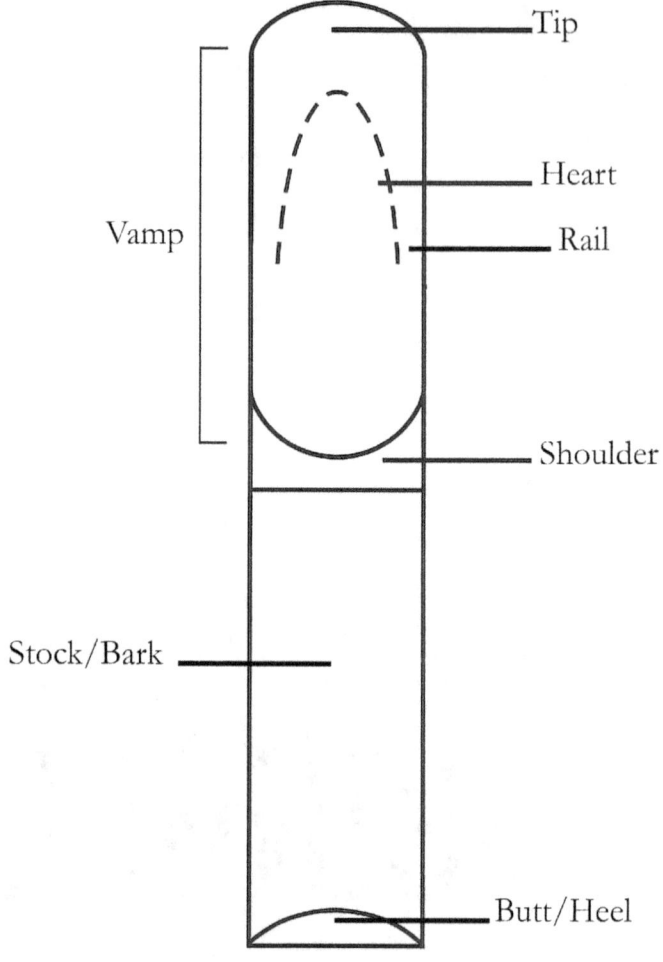

Figure SR-1 Reed Diagram.

reeds, on the contrary, have response issues in some or all of the range of the instrument, make controlling dynamics difficult, may cause inconsistent articulations, provide inappropriate (either too much or too little) wind resistance, and may lead to squeaks. Therefore, selecting and maintaining reeds is crucial for single reed players.

When many band directors think about selecting single reeds, they predominantly envision reed strength. Higher reed strength does not always equate to better sounds and advanced players do not "need" harder reeds. Instead, reed strength should be matched to the embouchure and mouthpiece of each individual student. Keep in mind that all reed strength suggestions are simply that: suggestions. Whereas reed strength, or the vague estimate of reed tip resistance, can be an important aspect of reed selection, several other factors contribute to the quality of a reed. Some of these factors can be evaluated by holding the reed up to a strong light, as doing so will highlight the shape of the heart. Ideally, the heart is centered on the reed and even in thickness, which can be seen as evenness of the darker colored vertical section in the middle of the vamp. If the heart is not centered (one side or the other is too thick or the shoulders are not equivalent) the reed may produce a hollow sound. Holding the reed to a light also allows an individual to evaluate the evenness of the tip. Finally, the vamp regularly begins with a U-shaped cut, which should be centered and even across the reed.

Single Reeds

As most reeds are machine cut and packaged, it is common to have wide fluctuations in quality inside each box. To that end, care and adjustment of reeds may maximize the quality of sounds students produce. At the beginner level, the most important initial considerations are to rotate reeds consistently and to dry them off prior to storing them in an appropriate storage device (most likely a dedicated reed guard). Students should label reeds (three to four reeds in rotation at a time) to keep track of their rotation and reeds should not be stored in the original reed case.

Furthermore, young students can be taught how to seal reeds with relative ease, which may extend reed lifespan (albeit at the cost of tone in some pedagogues' opinion). Begin by soaking the reed in water (not in the mouth), then lay the reed on a flat surface with the vamp/stock facing up. Then, rub a thumb along the vamp towards the tip three or four times and apply gentle pressure to seal the pores in the cane. Once the reed has dried, rub the back surface of the reed on the back of sandpaper or high stock printer paper. Finally, students may need to repeat the process a few more times before the reed is completely sealed. If students or teachers try reed sealing and find the tone quality significantly compromised, feel free to leave this out of beginning instruction.

More advanced students or performers may adjust their reeds for improved sound. Reeds that are too soft commonly produce edgy, bright tones and are more likely to fail in producing high notes. Hard reeds, in contrast, tend to produce fuzzy, spread tones and struggle to produce low notes. Of note, squeaks can be produced by reeds that are too soft OR too hard, because reed squeaks are the result of *uneven* reed vibrations. If a student continually squeaks and you have checked all other potential causes (of which there are many), hold their reed up to the light and look for symmetry in the heart, other dark lines in the shoulders, evenness in the tip, or warping.

Small adjustments are possible by adjusting the reed placement on the mouthpiece. If the reed is too soft, temporarily moving the reed closer to the mouthpiece tip will "harden" the reed and create stronger wind resistance, while moving the reed towards the instrument will "soften" the reed and decrease the wind resistance. This approach is limited, due to the dramatic changes in wind resistance and tone control that can be precipitated by over adjusting reed placement. Soft reeds can also be clipped with a dedicated reed trimmer to extend their lifespan or make adjustments to wind resistance and tone. Reeds that are too hard can be scrapped down with a reed knife or, in an emergency, can be sanded with 400- or 500-grit sandpaper.

MOUTHPIECE AND LIGATURE

Directors must also match reeds to mouthpieces. Single reed mouthpiece have three areas of concern: the facing, the tip opening, and the material (see Figure SR-2). The facing is the long section of the mouthpiece where the reed is secured, and contains the table (flat section with no hole) and the window (slightly curved section with a hole). Long facings require harder reeds, while short facings require softer reeds. The tip opening refers to the degree of curvature of the facing, or the distance between the tip of the mouthpiece and the tip of the reed. Open (larger) tip openings, like those of jazz mouthpieces, require softer reeds. Conversely, closed tip openings sound better with harder reeds. Finally, single reed mouthpieces come in a variety of materials. For classical tones and beginners, many teachers and performers prefer hard rubber mouthpieces to produce the best sounds. Some other mouthpieces, particularly jazz tenor and bari saxes, are made of metal. These mouthpieces project a brighter sound meant for playing solos or cutting through louder venues/ensembles. Avoid plastic mouthpieces whenever possible, as they produce poor tone quality and make proper intonation difficult.

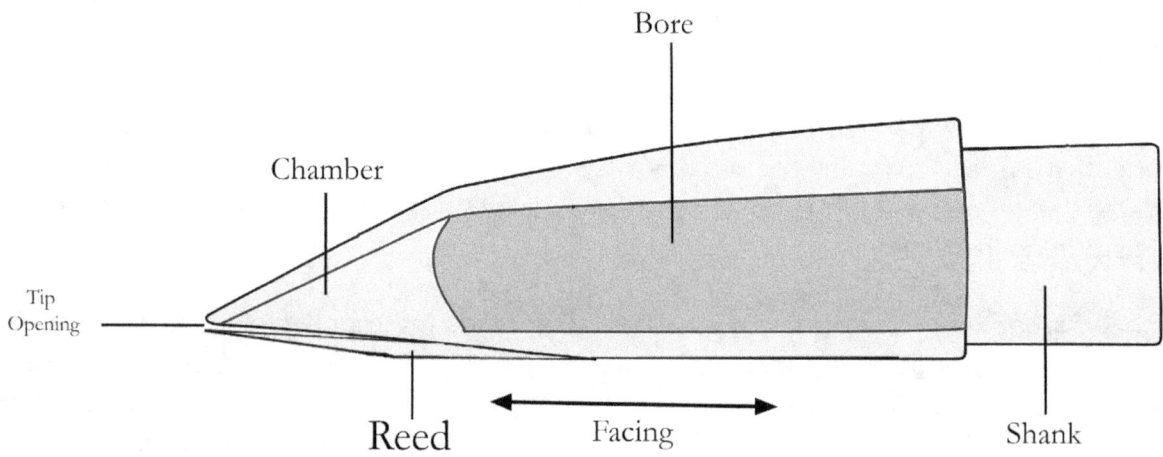

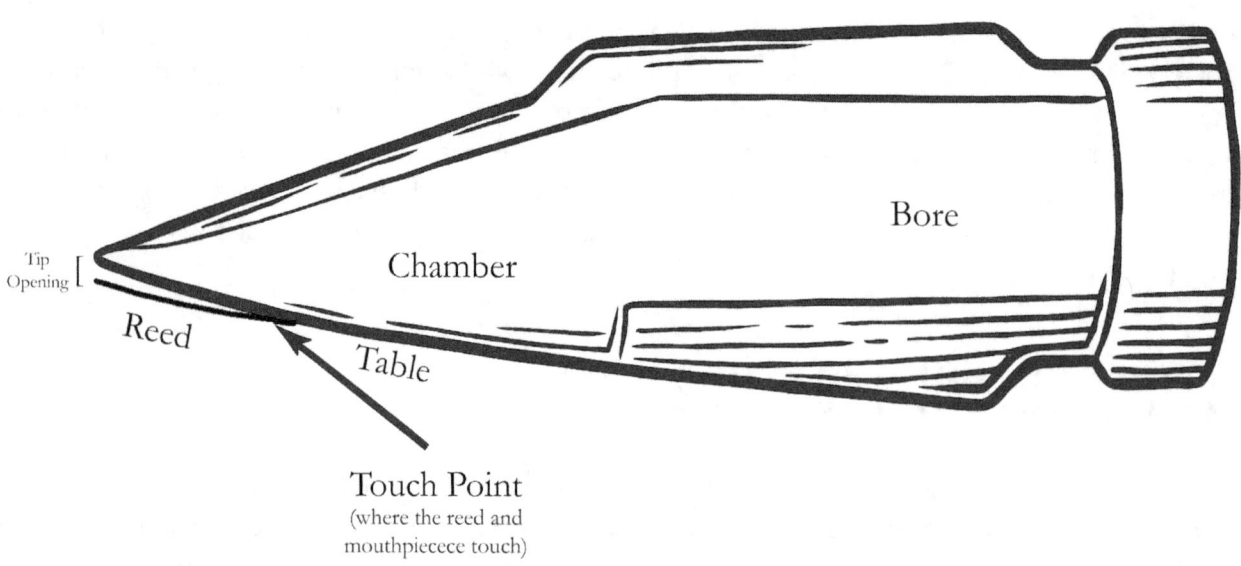

Figure SR-2 Mouthpieces

Single Reeds

Mouthpieces also require ligatures, and there exist many different ligature designs. Most models are made so that the tightening screw(s) are on the right of the mouthpiece whenever the instrument faces the player, regardless of whether the screw(s) are on the top or bottom. Metal ligatures are also conical (one ring is smaller than the other) and the larger ring should go onto the mouthpiece first so that the ligature slides down far enough to secure the reed. Manufacturers also make ligatures out of metal, cloth, or a combination of both and should be matched to the mouthpiece/reed combination and individual embouchure of the player. For beginners, Rovner, Bonade, and BG all make ligatures of consistent quality.

Both clarinet and saxophone have an ideal amount of mouthpiece that goes in the mouth; specifically, the part of the reed that is free to vibrate should be inside the mouth. Directors can use a note card to see where the reed touches/seals against the mouthpiece (Figure SR-3) and the teeth will rest on top.

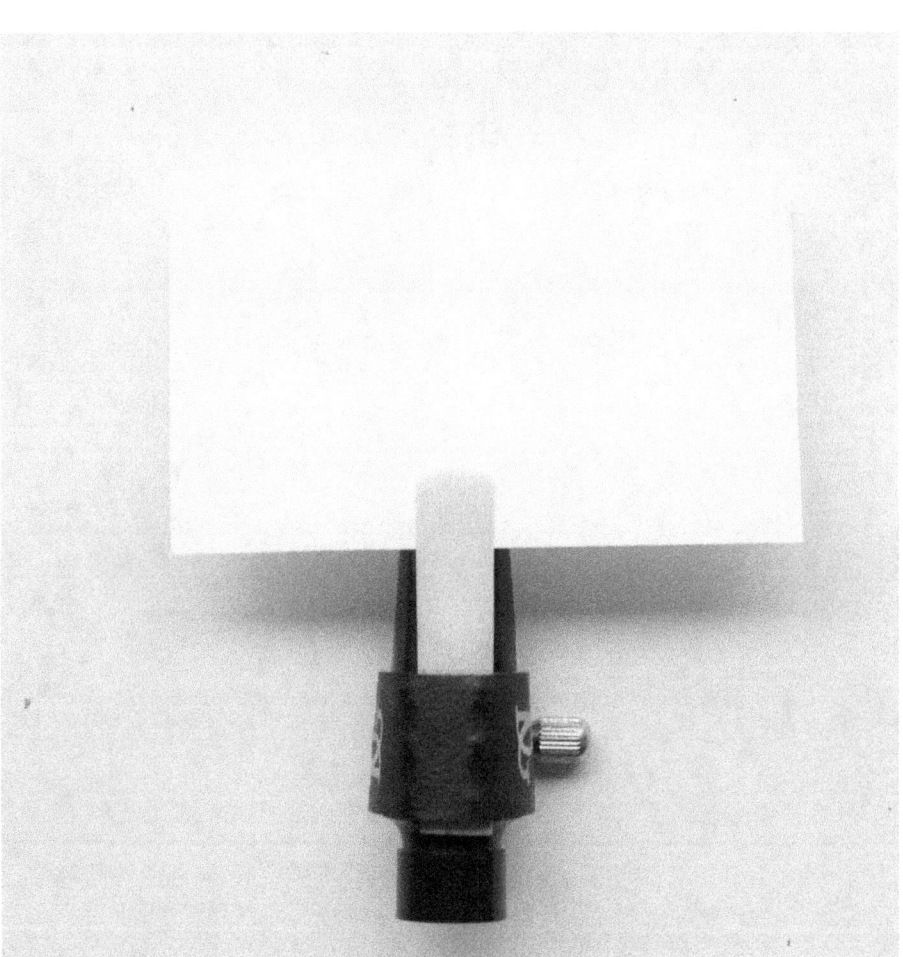

Figure SR-3 Reed Seal/Touch Point

CLARINET

Clarinet

The clarinet can trace its history back to the chalumeau, after which the first register is named. The modern version of the clarinet began approximately 1690, when Johan Christoph Denner developed the register key. Despite being accepted into the orchestra by the end of the Classical period, instrument makers continued to add keys to the clarinet until the general principals used in the creation of the modern flute were applied to clarinet by Eleonore Klose and August Buffet Jr around 1850. Fingerings for all the instruments in the clarinet family are essentially the same. The soprano and bass clarinet, the two clarinets most common in school bands, are both B-flat transposing instruments. Soprano clarinet sounds a whole step lower than written (Figure C-1).

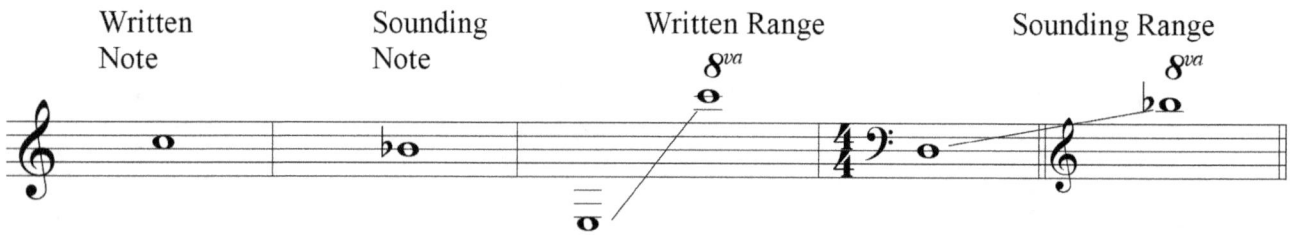

Figure C-1 Clarinet Range

While not rigid, below are approximate beginner, intermediate, and advanced ranges.

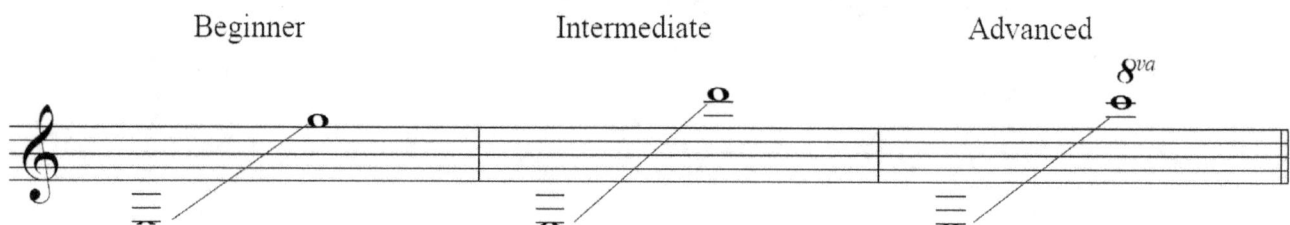

Figure C-2 Clarinet Skill Ranges

Bass clarinet sounds a 9th lower than written (Figure C-3).

Figure C-3 Bass Clarinet Range

Clarinet

The majority of this section will focus on the B-flat soprano clarinet, as that is the instrument most commonly taught to beginners.

INSTRUMENT SELECTION

When examining students for clarinet, begin with their teeth due to the important role teeth play in supporting the reed and therefore tone production. Even teeth are preferable for clarinetists and missing top front teeth can also impede student progress on the instrument. Look for students that have their front teeth (top and bottom) in alignment from both a teeth and jaw (overbite/underbite) perspective; although, students who are willing to make adjustments with their jaw can certainly still play the clarinet. Underbites are the most serious concern, as the angle that the clarinet enters the mouth can make underbites challenging (and sometimes painful) for students, especially as the bottom teeth support on the reed is an essential aspect of tone production.

Fingers are another area of consideration when selecting students for clarinet. The clarinet requires two physical finger characteristics for success: the ability to reach each of the keys and the ability to seal each of the tone holes. Look at the length of students' fingers, particularly Left Pinky and Right Pinky, and verify if they will be capable of depressing the necessary keys while maintaining proper finger position. While not a deal breaker, communicate clearly the concern regarding finger length for any interested student with short fingers. Similarly, students with long fingers can still play the clarinet, but directors should watch their finger shapes to avoid any unnatural positions or tension.

The ability to cover the tone holes, however, is of greater import. To form the first sounds on the instrument; student finger pads must be able to seal the tone holes. Finger 6 is worth specific attention, as it is the largest tone hole on the clarinet and students who are able to seal some of the other keys may still find this tone hole problematic. Check all student fingers to verify that they can seal the holes by having them hold the instrument correctly, squeezing their fingers on the hole and then lifting up for inspection. If there are complete circles (occasionally known as Cheerios), then the fingers are sealing. The ability to support the clarinet is often touted as an important factor, yet I believe this can be offset by the use of neck straps. Using neck straps also can be beneficial to students as it alleviates tension in the right hand and allows for easier development of right-hand position.

Finally, students with thick and thin lips can learn to play clarinet well. Wide lips (distance from corner to corner) may require students to exert more energy when bringing in their corners but are not a barrier to being selected for clarinet.

EQUIPMENT

In some band director positions, you will have the ability to influence the equipment your students procure for band class, which can be daunting on secondary instruments. Below are some suggestions for future reference that may change due to model updates and manufacturer quality. Additionally, do not hesitate to ask other band directors or private instructors for their recommendations. Intermediate and professional clarinets are made from grenadilla wood, however plastic models do exist that produce inferior tone quality. This list is simply a suggestion; good players can produce great sounds on a variety of equipment and need to find the right fit for their own bodies and situations.

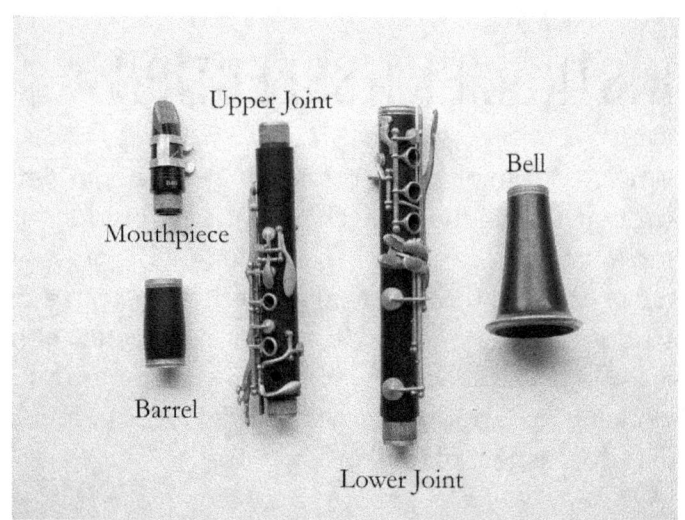

Figure C-4 Clarinet Parts

Instrument

Buffet E11 or Yamaha Advantage (wood) 400 or 450, LeBlanc Vito or Buffet Prodige (plastic/resin)

Mouthpieces

Beginners: Vandoren M15, 5RVLyre (slightly brighter), Fobes Debut, Upgrade: D'Addario x5 or x10

Ligature

Vandoren Leather LC21L, BG Revelation L4R (red cord), BG Super Revelation (green cord), Vandoren M/O Pewter LC51PP

Reeds

D'Addario Reserve Classic, Vandoren Classic (blue box)

Neck strap

Rico Clarinet Strap with thumb pad, BG Clarinet Support Strap

Clinet

ASSEMBLY

As discussed earlier, bent keys are most likely to occur during instrument assembly. Before putting the instrument together, be sure to address opening the case, naming the parts of the instrument, handling reeds, and greasing corks. It is worth noting that properly applying cork grease means putting some grease on the cork and then thoroughly rubbing it into the cork itself. The goal is for the grease to be absorbed by the porous cork for more consistent lubrication. Addressing all of these will save time and repair bills in the future.

Begin assembling the clarinet from the bell and work towards the mouthpiece. Check to see if all corks have been properly greased (small amount of grease rubbed into the cork) first, then hold the bell and lower joint on where there are no keys and gently twist the bell onto the lower joint. Next, grab the lower joint on the bottom in the back where there are no keys, pick up the upper joint with the palm touching the wood and fingers reaching around to depress the key that controls the bridge (Finger 2). Carefully twist the upper joint onto the lower joint, being careful to align the tone holes/key, especially the bridge key. As the barrel is conical, gently twist the large end of the barrel onto the upper joint, leaving a small gap between the barrel and upper joint, and then do the same for the mouthpiece. New tenon corks often need greasing, and students can place a small amount of cork grease on the corks, rub the grease into the corks, and then assemble the instrument. Over time, the need for greasing the corks will subside, and students will not need to put grease on every time.

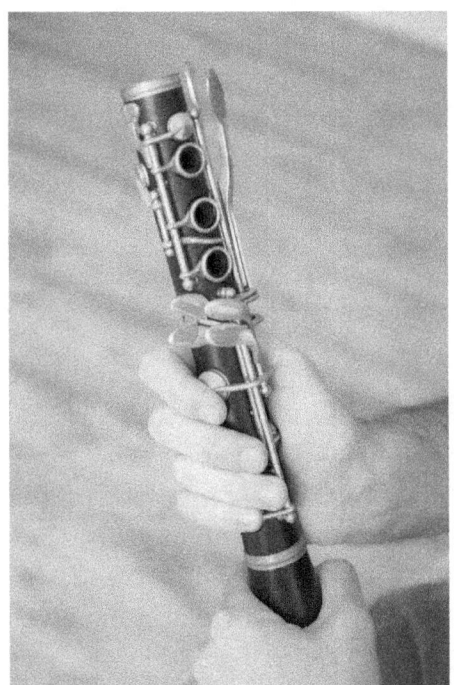
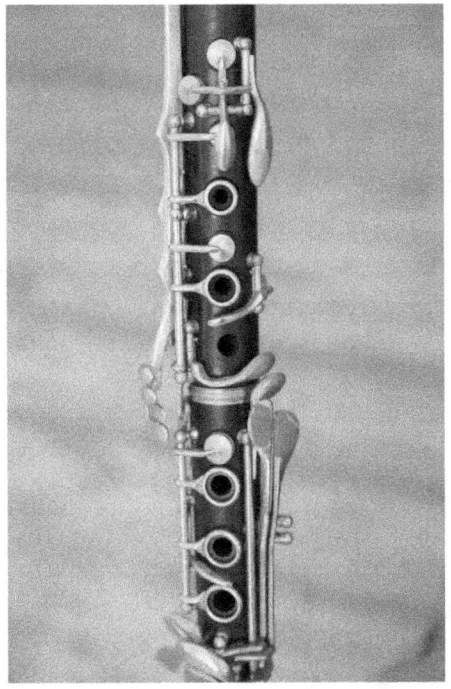

Figure C-5 Clarinet Assembly

Be sure to align the mouthpiece window with the register key on the upper joint, then place the ligature on the mouthpiece. Most clarinet ligatures are designed so that the screws will be operated with the right hand when looking at the mouthpiece window/reed. Finally, slide the reed onto the mouthpiece facing/table and secure the ligature. Of note, ligature placement can affect tone quality, as a higher placement on the mouthpiece will lead to a more closed tip opening. Many mouthpieces have a line to help students to find the appropriate ligature placement, but if not make sure that the ligature is low enough to expose a small amount of unshaved bark on the mouthpiece. Furthermore, ligatures should be secured, but not excessively tightened.

I often see students try to put their reed on before the ligature, but this presents a significant risk of chipped reeds. Teach students to put their ligature over the mouthpiece first, raise the ligature towards the tip to create space, then slide the reed against the mouthpiece table down into position. Taking time to put the reed on last will eventually save students, and their parents, money in replaced reeds.

TONE PRODUCTION AND EMBOUCHURE

After wind use (refer to the introduction for more info), embouchure is the core component of tone production, and in the case of the clarinet, the primary purpose of the embouchure is to facilitate proper reed vibration. To that end, embouchure cannot overcome a poor reed/mouthpiece/ligature. Regularly check student reeds for quality (warping, chipping, etc.). Furthermore, biting restricts reed vibration, and has no place in a desirable clarinet sound.

When conceptualizing clarinet embouchure, keep in mind three concepts: lips are energized around the mouthpiece/reed in all directions; lower teeth support the lip but do not provide extra pressure; and chin muscles should be flat and firm. Keep in mind that corners come in and generally down, never back and out. Sometimes students will hear "flat chin" and try to stretch their corners back instead of pulling muscles down towards their chin. To that end, my colleague Dr. Vanguel Tangarov, who teaches applied clarinet at Texas State University, prefers using the phrase "pointed chin" to be sure to draw the corners in and the chin down. The important thing to remember is that corners come near the canine teeth and set in/down, never back/up towards the ears.

Many novice students also struggle with maintaining equal lip energy and will tire quickly while correctly forming an embouchure in the early stages. The corners of the mouth are of singular concern, as these muscles are infrequently used compared to those of the jaw in daily life, and students often fall into the habit of applying jaw pressure to their embouchures instead of energizing the corners. Therefore, the first two points are connected; students who struggle to energize their lips evenly are those that frequently resort to teeth pressure. Finally, students can only have flat chin muscles when they avoid biting/teeth pressure with the bottom teeth.

Start teaching clarinet embouchure by practicing with the thumb. This allows them to have a greater tactile experience prior to using the mouthpiece/reed and they are less likely to bite down on their own hand. Begin by asking students to touch their bottom lip with the nail of their thumb (either hand is fine). The amount of bottom lip over the bottom teeth will depend on student lip thickness. Students with thick lips

Clarinet

will need less lip inside their mouth/underneath their thumb to approximate the appropriate embouchure. Ask them if they can feel their bottom teeth under their lips, then have them close their top teeth onto their thumb lightly. While double lip embouchures are definitely taught, I've always preferred for students to place their top teeth on the mouthpiece and I will get mouthpiece pads if students express any discomfort with the vibration on the top teeth rather than switch to double lip. That being said, if directors feel strongly about double lip take great care to watch the development of the bottom lip, the chin position, and the jaw pressure to avoid common complications. Finally, ask students to energize their lips around their thumb.

Another approach to get the general shape is to have students go through the above steps with a straw. Most children have blown bubbles through a straw before and energize their corners naturally when doing so; it can make for an easier approximation specifically of the corners while blowing. While I tend to use the thumb to get at the energized shape of the center of the lips and mouthpiece placement inside the mouth, I strongly encourage directors to experiment and find what works best with their students. With either approach, note that the bottom lip and teeth *support* the reed; they don't bite/press into it.

Once students have practiced with their thumbs, move on to the mouthpiece and reed. If possible, band directors should help each student individually with mouthpiece placement. Individual student factors, such as teeth, mouthpiece shape, and lip thickness can all influence proper mouthpiece placement, and these can be difficult for students to evaluate early in their playing career. A general rule for band directors is that the lower teeth should be slightly forward (towards the tip) of the point at which the reed and mouthpiece separate. For a clear idea of where this might be, slide an index card or business card between a mouthpiece and reed. The moment the card stops is the split point (see Figure SR-3). Bottom teeth should rest slightly towards the tip opening from this point. Another way to think of teeth placement is that teeth will rest approximately ½ inch from the tip.

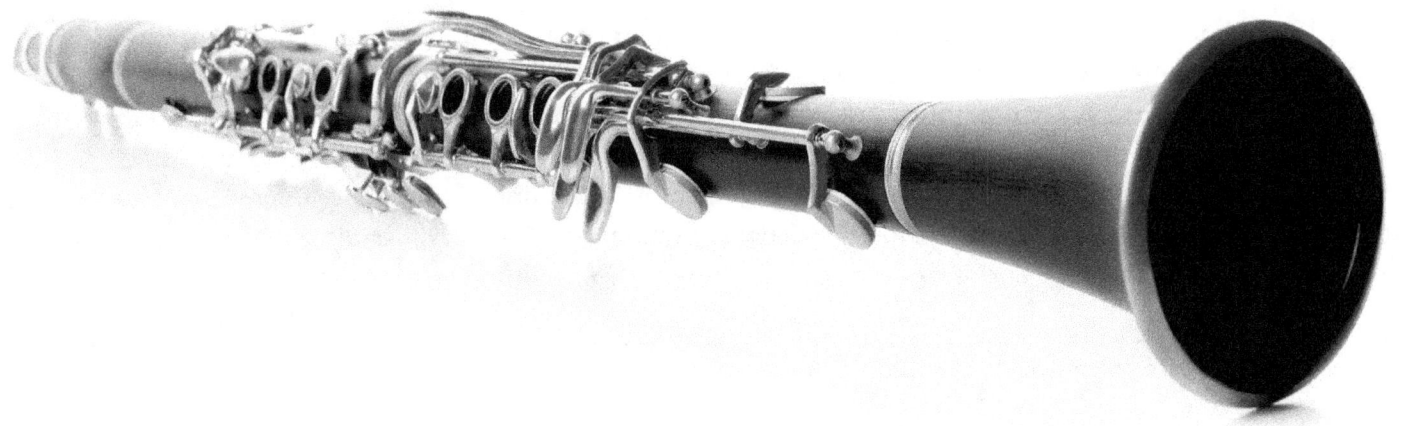

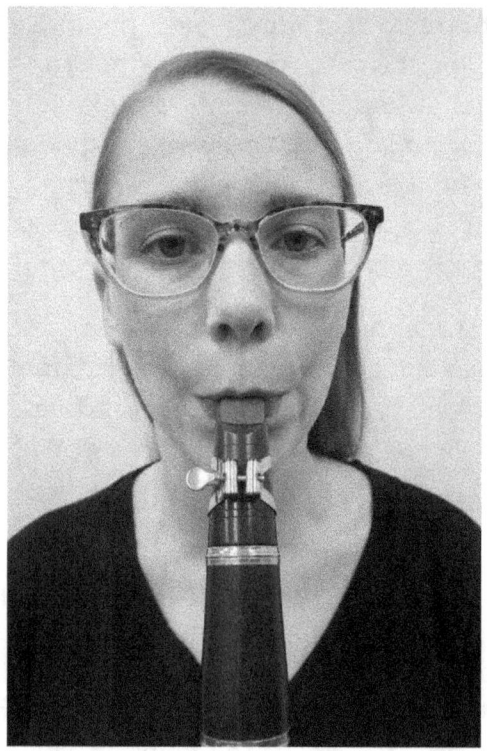 

Figure C-6 Clarinet Embouchure

Lastly, tongue placement inside the oral cavity affects both timbre and pitch on the clarinet.[1] Clarinetists tend to have higher tongue placement (think the syllable "ee") in the chalumeau and clarion registers, but have been found to drop the tongue as they move into the altissimo register.[2] When working with beginners, a former colleague typically asked students to say the syllables "ee-eew" to approximate both the tongue placement and the corner muscle energy used when playing the clarinet. I have found that this is another effective way to communicate and practice embouchure formation.

Despite discussing reeds earlier, it is worth stressing the importance of a good reed in the production of a good tone. Due to the machine-manufactured nature of reeds, each box will contain many poorly cut reeds that either need to be adjusted or thrown out. With beginners, directors can be a little more flexible regarding reed quality.

One question regarding clarinet reeds and beginners that comes up regularly is that of reed strength. There are widely divergent views as to the appropriate reed strength appropriate for starting students. Knowing the strengths are simply manufacturer estimates as to tip resistance/flexibility, I tend to start students on 2.5 or 3 strengths, depending on student wind and embouchure development. (More often I start them on 3.) If you choose to start students on 2.5 reeds (which I think is fine), know that you will want to move students to a harder reed as soon as their tone shows signs of edginess or spreading. The reasons for this are related to wind support and embouchure development. Students need consistent wind speed and

---

1   Gardener, 2010; Lulich, Charles, and Lulich, 2017
2   Lulich et al., 2017

Clarinet

pressure, as well as developed embouchure muscles that can be firm and still, to produce an ideal tone on the clarinet. Reeds that are too soft actually impede the development of these skills over time. Therefore, many beginners should be ready for 3.5 reeds going into their second year. I have worked with clarinetists who have consistently started their students on strength and moved to 3.5 relatively quickly and their students were quite successful as well as few who have started their beginners on 3.5 reeds right away, but I've also seen it done well with softer reeds. Essentially, the key is to monitor embouchure formation and tone production and move students to a thicker/harder reed when it is appropriate.

An important note for band directors is that squeaks are inevitable with beginning clarinetists. The vast panoply of potential causes ensure that students will, at some points, squeak. Students need to know that this is a natural part of learning the instrument, not a sign of abject failure. By being calm and informed, teachers can help students to learn the causes of squeaks and how to fix them faster than if excess emotion is brought to the event. Not all squeaks are caused by embouchure, so refer to the troubleshooting guide at the end of the chapter when performing triage on a serial squeaker.

EMBOUCHURE LESSON PLAN/INSTRUCTIONAL SEQUENCE

Subject: Clarinet   **Grade:** 6   **Date:**

- ♪ **Concept:**
  Making a characteristic tone on the mouthpiece and barrel

- ♪ **Behavioral Learning Objective:**
  Students will be able to form a characteristic embouchure and assess themselves or others regarding embouchure.

- ♪ **Standards:**
  MU:Pr5.3.E.5a/MU:Pr6.1.E.5a (National Standards example) or TEKS 117.208.C.3.B (State Standards example).

Vocabulary:
Embouchure, energize, chin

Materials:
Mouthpiece, barrel, reed, ligature

Time:
10–15 minutes

Clarinet

Procedures

1. Students draw their bottom lip slightly over their bottom teeth, so that the colored part of the lip is still visible.
2. Students place their thumbnail on their bottom lip, being careful to avoid rolling their lip further into their mouth.
3. Students wiggle their thumb to feel their teeth through the bottom lip.
4. Students close their top teeth to their thumb.
5. Students seal their lips around their thumb, energizing the lips uniformly around their thumb.
6. Assemble the mouthpiece/reed and barrel (always both, never mouthpiece alone).
7. Optional: Students say "ee-eew" to practice tongue position and corner muscle engagement.
8. Optional: Place mouthpiece and barrel into students' mouths, have them seal and blow with tongue in the "ee" position.
9. Teacher shows students bottom lip placement on reed.
10. Students place mouthpiece and barrel into mouth, close top teeth, seal lips, and blow wind (resulting pitch should be F-sharp—ideally between +10 and +35 cents sharp)
11. Students assess themselves in the mirror and compare to teacher model/ideal image.

ASSESSMENT

Evaluate embouchure by comparing to an ideal image of clarinet embouchure, check sounding pitch with a tuner (sharp F-sharp is ideal).

ARTICULATION

Like all wind instruments, proper wind support is necessary for correct articulation. Only the tip of the tongue is used to articulate, and the tongue acts as a release valve for the wind at the start of a note. On clarinet, **the tip of the top of the tongue touches the tip of the bottom of the reed**. I use this tongue twister with my students, and we turn it into a chant that helps them remember the ideal tongue to reed connection when heavy tongues creep into their performance. To clarify, when I demonstrate articulation to the students I also identify where the "tip" and "bottom" of the reed are for me, which means the thin part of the reed on the curved/shaved side. Excessive tongue pressure against the reed or too much tongue/reed contact will lead to hard, aggressive attacks. Furthermore, only the tip of the tongue moves during articulation. Beginners are prone to disproportionate tongue movements or moving their jaws as they articulate.

Motion is the enemy of beginning clarinet embouchures. Students need to both know that maintaining a consistent and correct embouchure is important for success and have opportunities to practice keeping still while tonguing. Regularly work mouthpiece/barrel articulation exercises, fast tonguing on the entire instrument, etc. to help them build the muscle control to move the arched tongue correctly while keeping the embouchure still.

Clarinet

Always begin articulation instruction with connected wind and unmetered tongue movement. This allows students to concentrate on using the tip of the tongue while maintaining wind and embouchure. Remember; every time you add a new performance element or skill, students tend to struggle to maintain proficiency in the previously learned skills. After introducing the tongue motion and placement, move to metered articulation exercises.

ARTICULATION LESSON PLAN AND INSTRUCTIONAL SEQUENCE

Subject: Clarinet   **Grade:** 6   **Date:**

♪ **Concept:**
Articulating correctly on a variety of rhythms

♪ **Behavioral Learning Objective:**
Students will be able to perform articulated notes in a variety of rhythms while maintaining proper embouchure.

♪ **Standards:**
MU:Pr5.3.E.5a/MU:Pr6.1.E.5a/ MU:Pr4.2.E.5a (National Standards example) or TEKS 117.208.C.3.B (State Standards example)

 **Vocabulary:**
Articulation, tonguing, quarter notes, stability, legato

 **Materials:**
Mouthpiece, barrel, reed, ligature, white/chalk board, entire instrument (optional)

 **Time:**
15–20 minutes

Procedures

1. Students play an F# on the mouthpiece & barrel

2. Students touch top of the tip of the tongue to the bottom of the tip of the reed

3. (Optional) Teacher models syllable "tee" for students and students repeat – teacher points students' attention to tongue placement

4. Students blow wind and move their tongue without the mouthpiece & barrel – teacher assesses wind consistency

5. Teacher models unmetered articulation for students

6. Students blow wind and move their tongue with proper embouchure on mouthpiece & barrel – unmetered practice

7. Teacher models metered quarter notes – full value

8. Students perform quarter notes on mouthpiece & barrel (be sure to watch/listen for students who are cheating by using a breath or "who" start)

129

PLAYING POSITION

Holding the clarinet involves the right thumb (or neck strap) and top teeth. Students' Right Thumb should support the instrument with the thumb pad in contact with the lower joint and the thumb rest sitting between the tip and first knuckle. Smaller or younger students may be tempted to rest the bell on their legs/knees; avoid this at all costs due to the impact it has on mouthpiece placement and posture. I strongly encourage band directors to have their beginners use neck straps if students are struggling to hold the instrument correctly, as they considerably alleviate the weight on the right thumb, thus allowing students to develop correct finger positions in their right hand while maintaining proper mouthpiece placement. All fingers should remain slightly curved, with the finger pads facing towards the instrument (as they need to seal the tone holes). The left thumb should however at a 1 o'clock position by the F and register keys, while directors should check right thumbs to make sure that students keep the thumb rest over their first knuckle and that the thumbnail somewhat faces the student.

Remember, students need to bring the instrument to their face, so carefully watch for students who either drop their chins or slouch their backs to reach when playing. Both actions restrict wind flow; however lowered chins will also affect reed vibration/jaw pressure and therefore change tone, intonation, and create squeaks. Top teeth should be in contact with the mouthpiece, and I have found that mouthpiece pads help young students to set their teeth to the mouthpiece without biting or sliding.

Figure C-7 Clarinet Playing Position

In general, students should hold the clarinet at an angle somewhere between 30°–40°. Instrument angles will depend largely on teeth shape and placement, posture, and where the sound is most resonant. To find the appropriate position for each student, have the student begin with the instrument too close to his or her body and play a sustained note while slowly moving the clarinet to a greater angle. At the point where the sound is the most resonant, have the student stop and look at themselves in the mirror; this is their ideal playing position. Do not attempt this procedure until students are consistently producing an F-sharp on their mouthpiece and barrel. Don't let music stands or posture create poor instrument angles or tone will suffer; move music stands or have students play standing up to ensure that they are holding the instrument correctly.

Figure C-8 Clarinet Hand Position

INTONATION

Intonation on clarinet is primary created by wind support, mouthpiece/reed, and embouchure. Without these things, tuning the instrument by mechanical means is extremely difficult. With beginners, greater time and focus on the sources of intonation problems will better serve student performance. When tuning the instrument, the primary method is barrel placement, with a larger gap between the barrel and upper joint lowering the pitch (flat) and a smaller gap raising the pitch (sharp). Adjusting the barrel has a greater effect on notes where the first open hole is closer to the mouthpiece than those where the first open note is closer to the bell. The clarinet can be tuned using the following notes (Figure C-9):

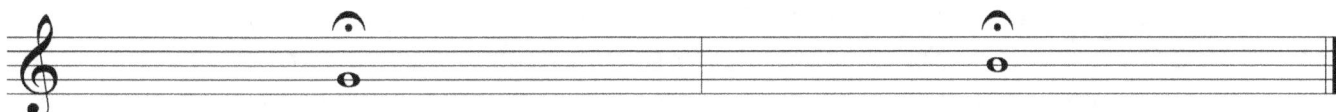

Figure C-9 Clarinet Tuning Notes

Additionally, the following notes some of the more egregious notes on the clarinet in terms of intonation (Figure C-10):

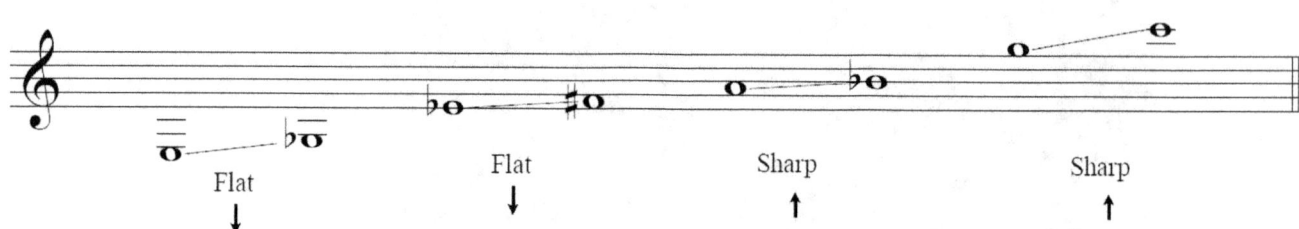

Figure C-10 Clarinet Intonation Challenges

Several aspects of the mouthpiece/reed affect intonation. Reeds that are too hard tend to play sharp, while those that are too soft tend to play flat. Furthermore, the amount of mouthpiece in the mouth and playing position angle can also influence tuning. Too little mouthpiece tends to produce flat sounds, while too much mouthpiece often plays sharp. Likewise, too large a playing angle (bell too far from body) leads to flat sounds and too small a playing angle (bell too close to the body) plays sharp.

All wind instruments have intonation considerations when changing dynamics. During crescendos, the clarinet tends to drift flat. Conversely, the clarinet is inclined to play sharp during decrescendos. Players can use their embouchures/tongue placement to offset both tendencies, provided they have solid embouchure control and are aware of the proclivities of the instrument.

TECHNICAL CONSIDERATIONS

There are three technical issues on clarinet with which I believe all band directors should familiarize themselves. One of the technical aspects overlooked by inexperienced teachers is that of how students move Finger 1. Unlike most of the other primary fingers (2–6), Finger 1 is responsible for multiple keys. Furthermore, they keys differ, as the A and A-flat keys do not have tone holes, while the E key does. Students *must* be taught to roll their finger from the E key to the A/A-flat keys. This motion often feels unnatural to students, and directors would be wise to practice the motion often through various exercises and songs. Most dedicated clarinet methods contain a section dedicated to building the roll (or rock) motion. Additionally, students like to stack fingers when rolling (i.e., place Finger 2 on top of the rolled Finger 1 or press Fingers 2 and 3 together), which should also be addressed immediately before the habit takes root.

Most notes that involve the pinky keys can be played two different ways. Fortunately, the rule is simple: alternate pinkies whenever possible. Make sure to clearly teach both fingerings for pinky notes as well as require students to demonstrate mastery of both fingerings through various technique exercises.

Clarinet

The technical issue that creates the most anxiety in non-clarinetists is the register change, commonly referred to as "crossing the break." Before discussing the nature of register changes and how to teach them effectively, there are a couple of pieces of advice I would like to give. The first is to reiterate that squeaks on the beginning clarinet are inevitable. The more the teacher emotionally reacts to squeaks, the more tense the students become regarding them, which ironically will often increase the frequency of squeaks in performance. Many students grow up in a failure-averse environment already; do not add fuel to that fire by being surprised or bothered by something that I guarantee will happen (and has happened to all of the best clarinetists in the world when they were beginners). Secondly, do not approach register changes as something "hard" or "scary." Notice how I have not used the typical "crossing the break" terminology? This is intentional, as I would like readers to realize that even naming something in a scary way can increase tension or fear. Learning to change registers is no different from learning to make a great sound on G or articulating with the tip of the tongue. If the teacher is calm and has an appropriate sequence, student success will follow.

The clarinet has three primary registers: chalumeau, clarion, and altissimo (Figure C-11). The first two registers are extremely similar in how performers use their embouchure and wind, therefore learning register changes effectively starts with proper mastery of the chalumeau register. Students who have flat chins, energized lips, and a slightly arched tongue over which they move steady, fast wind are already well on their way to successfully playing in the clarion register.

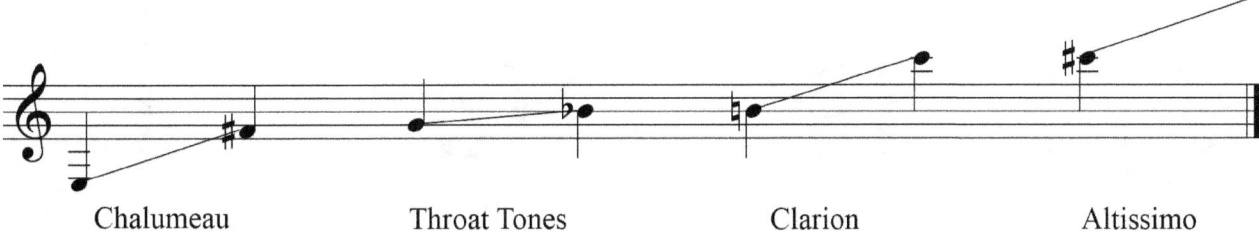

Figure C-11 Clarinet Registers

That leaves fingers as the only other hurdle to the first register change. To help build quick and comfortable right hand finger shifts, I teach resonance fingerings prior to register changes. For those unfamiliar, from G4–B-flat4 students can add Fingers 4, 5, and 6 as well as Left Pinky on the F key (see Figure C-12) and the correct note will still sound. By introducing and practicing these fingerings, teachers are building in the right-hand movements necessary to cross registers diatonically, for example from A4 to B4. Similar to other alternate fingerings, students should not learn *only* the resonance fingerings. However, I have found them useful for building the muscle memory necessary for smooth register changes.

It is worth noting that some clarinet pedagogues are strongly against resonance fingerings for primarily two reasons: using resonance fingerings all the time can create habits that do not transfer to every situation, and resonance fingerings change pitch/timbre. Both are legitimate concerns and so, like with alternate fingerings used for technical passages, directors should use resonance fingerings intentionally and vary their use to avoid bad habits. Know that if directors choose not to use these fingerings, they must still find ways to help students build the skill of adding Fingers 4, 5, 6, and Right Pinky quickly, appropriately (covering holes completely), and in unison.

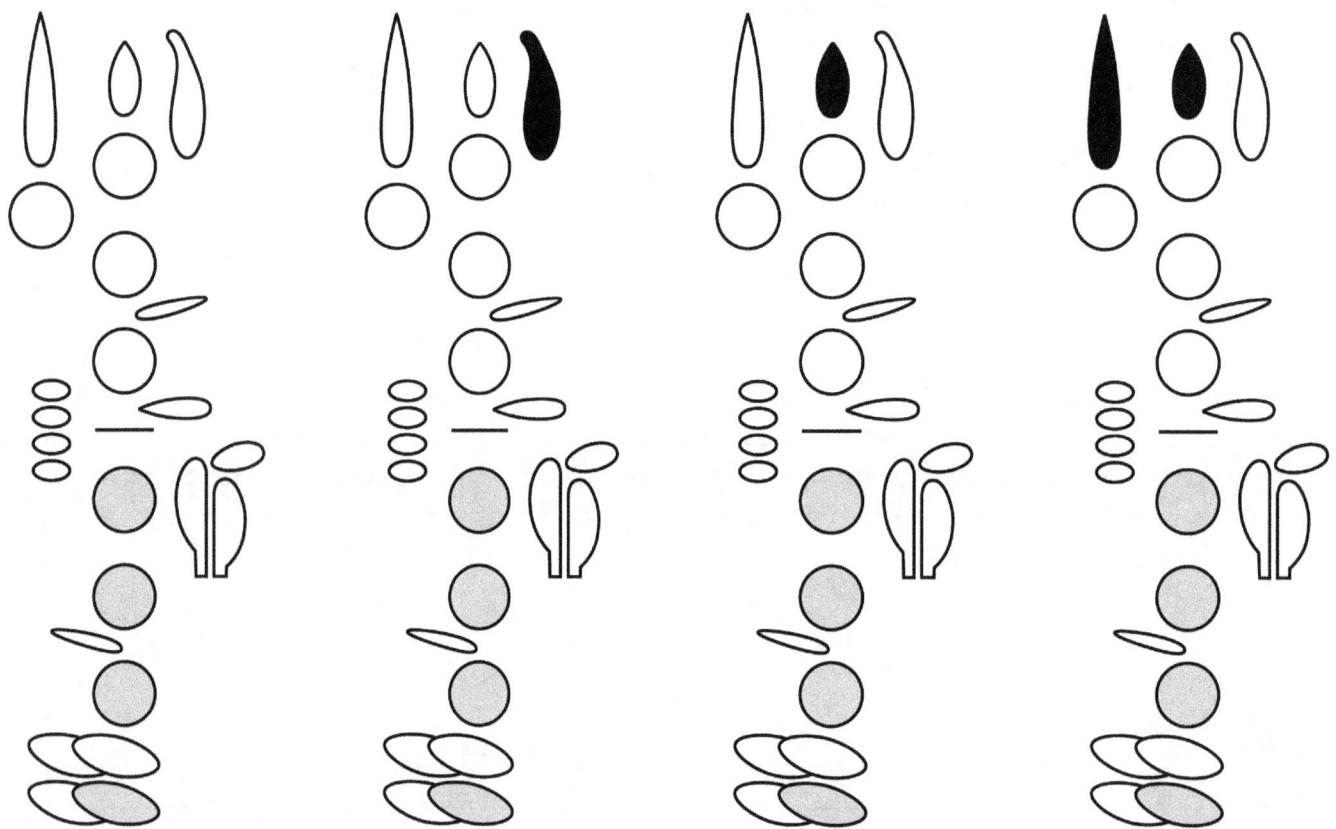

Figure C-12 Resonance Fingerings

Once students have established both a consistent chalumeau tone and have developed muscle memory in their right hand, teachers can begin to practice register changes. The best way to verify that students are ready is to ask them to play a note lower in the chalumeau register and you then press the register key. If embouchure, tongue placement, wind, and reeds are all appropriate, the register will change automatically. I always perform this check prior to teaching register changes, even in large or heterogeneous classes. Too many bad habits and frustrating experiences can materialize if teachers introduce register changes before students are ready. If the sound does not change registers immediately (instead making a fuzzy, honking sound) check the performance pitch on the mouthpiece and barrel. Often students will either have poor bottom lip/teeth use or their tongues will be far too low in their mouths, both of which will result in lower mouthpiece and barrel pitch (remember, a slightly sharp F-sharp is ideal).

Clarinet

If all the students produce the clarion notes with the teacher pressing the register key, they are ready to learn to change registers themselves. Pay attention to the LT, as it should be hovering at a 1 o'clock position, nearly parallel to the clarinet itself. It is imperative that students can seal the F key with their thumb and rock to the register key without breaking the seal. Furthermore, stress to students that everything must remain the same from chalumeau to clarion register except for the register key. Students are prone to trying to increase jaw pressure or wind speed to make the higher notes sound, which actually works against their success. The first two registers of the clarinet are all about stability and consistency: wind should stay the same, embouchure should stay the same, fingers need to seal the tone holes the same way, etc. At this point, use the notation to slur across the register using only the register key. Every solid method book will have lines dedicated specifically to this exercise. As slurs become more consistent, add articulations on the clarion notes. Finally, work diatonic changes across the register in the form of scale patterns and music.

Lastly, directors should introduce students to the pinky keys during their beginner experience in a logical and thought-out manner. Students need to understand the alternate fingerings and when to use them. I have used colored stickers (i.e., both keys for F have a blue sticker). However, I know many teachers who assign the keys numbers. Any approach that allows students to ascertain which pinky key the teacher is referring to and make the connections between which pinky keys produce the same sound is perfectly acceptable. Assess students' knowledge on general fingerings and which fingerings are alternates for the same notes, prior to teaching the situations to use each fingering. For those unfamiliar with the instrument, *the general rule is that the same pinky should not press two different keys sequentially*. Therefore, in contrast to saxophone, students should never slide pinkies between keys.

THE CLARINET FAMILY

The instruments of the clarinet family are all transposing instruments with the same general key structure/fingerings. Additionally, all clarinets have the same basic written range, even though sounding ranges vary, and the family can be split into higher (E-flat soprano, A, and B-flat soprano) and lower (alto, B-flat bass, and contrabass) groups. In most beginning band programs, directors will focus on the B-flat soprano and B-flat bass clarinets; however, the others regularly appear in more advanced literature.

Successfully performing on an E-flat soprano clarinet presents several challenges. The entire instrument is smaller, and therefore embouchures must be more *stable* and energized while the fingers navigate such close key work. Tiny changes in embouchure can lead to extensive changes in sound and pitch on the E-flat soprano. Furthermore, the smaller tip opening combined with taking less mouthpiece in the mouth creates considerably more wind resistance than on a standard B-flat soprano.

The A clarinet shares many similarities with the B-flat soprano, and students who are successful on the latter should be able to transition to the former with relative ease. For instance, both A and B-flat clarinets use the same mouthpiece and reed, and therefore the embouchures start from the same basic point. This is not to say that there are no differences between the instruments, yet when even the bore diameters are the same, one would be forgiven for asking why even have the A clarinet at all. The answer lies largely in the history of the instrument, from a time when key systems and instrument intonation were less developed, and players needed multiple instruments to perform in multiple keys successfully.

Clarinet

All of the low clarinets (E-flat alto, E-flat contralto, B-flat bass, and B-flat contrabass) have a curved neck, curved bell, and a half-hole option for Finger 1. These instruments share many considerations, and I will address them as a group (henceforth referred to as *low clarinets*). The low clarinets are all bigger than their higher counterparts and require extraneous means of support in the forms of neck straps and end pins/floor pegs. When seated, students should hold the low clarinets between their legs, centered in the middle of their body and the bell should be slightly closer to the student's body, so that the correct mouthpiece angle is preserved.

Some models of low clarinets have tunable necks (the neck has a telescopic insert) that allows for greater tuning flexibility; however, with most student models you are left with the small adjustments that can be made at the base of the neck itself. As such, embouchure, wind use, and tongue placement are essential for playing the low clarinets in tune. Of note, the oral cavity tends to open up the lower the instrument in comparison to B-flat soprano. So, students who switch to contrabass clarinet will have to use a more open oral cavity that may feel natural at first.

Finally, the larger mouthpiece/reed combination means a larger tip opening, which in turn provides less wind resistance than high clarinets. Many students who switch from soprano to bass will try to maintain reed strength in some misconstrued idea that the higher number equals greater skill (hint: it does not equal skill...at all). Students who produce an excessively fuzzy or weak tone may very well be on a reed that is too hard for their mouthpiece/embouchure.

IDEAL AURAL IMAGES

1. Lian Wang
2. Sabine Meyer
3. Jon Manasse
4. Peter Cigleris
5. Anthony McGill
6. Karl Leister
7. Robert Marcellus
8. Daniel Bonade
9. Jae Hee Choi
10. Paul Meyer
11. Florent Heau

Clarinet

SELECTED RESOURCES

For Clarinets Only — by Mattei, published by Mattei Music Services

So You Want to Play the Clarinet — by Corley, published by Southern/Hal Leonard

How to Play Clarinet in 14 Days: Daily Lessons for Absolute Beginners —Austria and Nelson, published by Troy Nelson Music

The Break: Mastering the Middle Register of the Clarinet — by Corley, published by Southern/Hal Leonard

Rubank Elementary Method — by Hovey, published by Hal Leonard

Complete Method for Clarinet — by Baermann, published by Alfred

PRACTICAL TIPS

Assembly

- Always open the case on the floor.
- Assemble from the bottom up.
    - Bell first/reed last.
- Watch for the bridge key between lower and upper joints.
- Never place the barrel flush to the upper joint—even for beginners.
- In contrast, always make sure the mouthpiece is flush on the barrel.
- Reeds are last on, first off.
    - Have the ligature already on the mouthpiece. Trust me, students will clip reeds trying to slide the ligature over the mouthpiece and reed together. Don't let them try it.
- Reeds should be aligned with the tip of the mouthpiece.
    - My go-to for telling when they are aligned is to see black at the tip when looking at the reed and see reed at the tip when looking at the top of the mouthpiece.
    - Never let them touch the tip of the reed to check placement (or for any other reason).
    - Reed placement can greatly impact tone—check students regularly.
- Grip the clarinet from the back or the keys, never the rods.

Clarinet

- Ligatures need to go down far enough on the mouthpiece to be past the line of bark on the reed.
  - Ligatures are conical, so make sure that it can slide far enough down the mouthpiece.
- Never tighten ligatures all the way, just enough until you feel resistance is sufficient.
  - Overtightening restricts reed vibration.
- Ligature screws are almost always on the right side, but can be on the top or bottom of the ligature.
- Cork grease must be rubbed into new corks. (You can tell by the color—light brown is less greased.)

Embouchure

- Too much mouthpiece leads to squeaks.
  - If you're unsure how much mouthpiece students should have in their mouth, try sliding a piece of paper between the reed and mouthpiece, where it stops is a good estimate of the line between inside and outside of the mouth.
- Too little mouthpiece leads to thin tones or no tone at all.
- **Constantly** assess for flat chin.
  - Use mirrors to allow students to assess their own flat chins.
- The reed needs a firm cushion to vibrate properly.
  - Too soft bottom lips lead to a wide variety of tone problems.
  - Bottom lip positions will vary slightly depending on students' lip shape.
  - Bottom lips shouldn't be sucked completely into the face (no denture lips).
- Corners come in (near canine teeth).
  - Don't allow puffy cheeks.
- Mouthpiece savers can make the top teeth more comfortable but watch for biting.
- As much as you can, have all beginners play on the same mouthpiece/ligature setup.
- Tongues need to be raised proper tone and intonation. (I consider this part of the embouchure for clarinet because it is equally important.)
- Correct embouchure (specifically crescent through the bottom lip, bottom teeth, and chin) and tongue placement should produce an F-sharp on the mouthpiece and barrel. (Shoot for 10 to 35 cents sharp—being a little on the sharp side is good.)

Clarinet

- While I teach top teeth touching the mouthpiece, some teachers use double lip for beginners.
    - Regardless of the difference on the top, the crescent on the bottom is paramount for tone.
- Missing or crooked front teeth (especially bottom) can prove to be extremely challenging for embouchure formation.
- Energy needs to be applied from all directions around the mouthpiece/reed.
    - Teachers typically tell students to make it even or round, which works well, but know that more advanced players tend to put slightly more energy into the crescent (corners, bottom lip, chin, bottom teeth) than with the top lip/teeth.
    - Some students will not have enough energy from the top lip. Make sure students are sealing the wind and supporting the mouthpiece.
- Bottom jaw pressure is one of the easier things to assess on the mouthpiece/barrel, but is not the sole determinant of tone quality.
- Stillness is crucial for beginning clarinet embouchures.
    - It takes time to build the muscle strength necessary to hold the embouchure still—so be patient and give students breaks.

Articulation

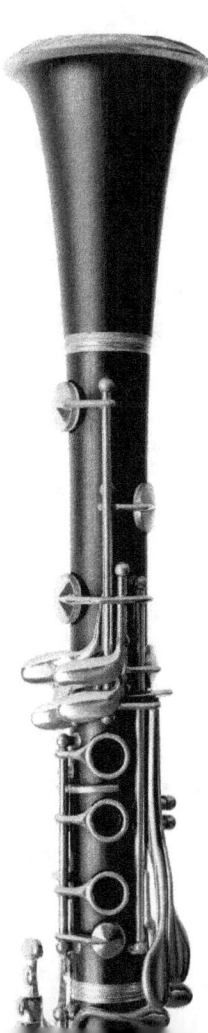

- Proper wind and embouchure are necessary for articulation; do not teach articulation until these are relatively well established.
- Tip of the top of the tongue touches the tip of the bottom of the reed.
- Fast tongue movements, even on slow notes.
- Let students experiment and work to match attack/articulation sound with a model.
- Keep the tongue raised.
- Try to avoid anchor tonguing (putting the tip of the tongue against the bottom teeth and moving the middle of the tongue) when possible.
- Tonguing does not stop the reed from vibrating.
- Wind flows out when playing, in when breathing only. Articulation is more like waving a hand across an open faucet of water; the water never stops nor should the wind.

Clarinet

Playing Position

- Right thumb holds the weight of the instrument.
  - Thumbnail pointed towards the player.
  - First knuckle supporting the thumb rest.
  - Don't be afraid to use extra padding or neck straps to help students maintain correct hand position with their right hand.
- Bells should not rest on the legs/knees—if the weight is that big of a problem use a neck strap.
- Clarinets generally are held at a 30°–45° angle.
  - Heads should never move to the clarinet; the angle of the mouthpiece in the mouth is important for tone.
  - Teeth and lips can make for slight differences in angle from student to student. Choose the angle with the best sound.
- Fingers need to hover over the keys.
  - This is, in my opinion, even more important for clarinet than the other woodwinds because the holes must be completely sealed to avoid squeaks.
  - Fingers need to be high enough to vent, but not so removed from the keys that students have a hard time finding their fingerings later.
- Left thumb slightly offset from parallel.
  - Approximately 1–2 o'clock (similar to oboe).
  - Needs to be able to reach the register key.
  - Left thumb hovers like the other fingers, not placed on the instrument like sax.
- Finger 1 needs to be curved so that it can reach the A/A-flat keys.
  - This finger needs to *roll* between the first tone hole and A/A-flat keys. Do not let students lift it back and forth between the fingerings.
- Watch out for stacked fingers (where the fingers touch each other).
- Finger 4 needs special attention to make sure it doesn't stray from home; it is responsible for the side keys later on in the semester.
- Use neck straps to relieve thumb tension when necessary.
- Too little mouthpiece leads to no/weak sounds.
- Too much mouthpiece leads to squeaks.

Other Tips

- ♪ The break doesn't have to be scary, provided you have sequenced everything well leading up to it.
  - ⊙ Build up the composite skills first (embouchure, tongue placement, wind, articulation, moving the right-hand fingers together, rolling to throat tones, etc.).
  - ⊙ Be sure students can produce an F-sharp prior to entering into the clarion register.
  - ⊙ Repetition is necessary to ensure the composite skills are automatized.
  - ⊙ Be patient with students and don't make crossing the break a big deal emotionally.
  - ⊙ As soon as their skills are solid, start with register key exercises.
  - ⊙ While I am a big believer in practicing resonance fingerings (right hand down), not everyone agrees that the intonation trade-offs are worth it for beginners.
    - If directors choose not to use resonance fingerings, be sure to make students practice moving all right-hand fingers in unison prior to crossing the break.
- ♪ Stillness is helpful for beginning clarinetists. Work to develop embouchures that are correct AND don't move around.
- ♪ Technique comes easier than tone; don't rush ahead if they can't control their sound.
- ♪ Woodwind technique is largely making students do a large variety of technical patterns a ridiculous number of times.
- ♪ Throat tones are difficult to make sound good and play in tune, even for dedicated performers.
- ♪ Practice finger patterns to give faces a break early in the year.
- ♪ Have a system for labeling pinky keys and use it consistently.
- ♪ Reeds matter!
  - ⊙ Reed rotations are necessary—insist on a bare minimum of three working reeds (five preferable).
  - ⊙ Check reeds often; don't assume students are on top of reed rotations, maintenance, or placement during their beginner experience.
  - ⊙ Not all reeds that come from a box are created equal.
- ♪ Tone on clarinet is largely correct embouchure and tongue placement combined with a quality reed matched to the perfect mouthpiece/ligature and supported by proper wind.
- ♪ Intonation is complicated.
  - ⊙ Consistent tone is a prerequisite for effective intonation.

- Reeds matter with intonation too.
- So does everything else (embouchure, mouthpiece model/shape, ligature, tongue position, wind support, etc.).
- Mechanical adjustments of pitch happen primarily at the barrel.
- Mouthpiece shape and barrel length/shape can also affect tuning significantly.
  - Mouthpieces and barrels come in varying bore diameters—they have to be matched to the instrument for more advanced intonation.

♪ Swabbing will make pads last longer.
- Non-silk swabs get caught on a metal insert near the top of the upper joint easily. Use silk when possible.
- Don't use pad savers; they just trap moisture by the pads and shorten their lifespan.

♪ Force correct repetitions of difficult finger combinations.
- Anything shifting to or from throat tones
- Pinkies

BEGINNER CLARINET SEQUENCE EXAMPLE

The sequence listed below is a suggestion and is not meant to be exhaustive or perfect. Instead, this sequence should serve as a leaping-off point for directors to plan their own beginner courses. Also, keep in mind that many of the items, particularly at the beginning, will happen concurrently. This is due, in part, to the fact that students will not have the physical or mental endurance to spend an entire class on one topic or content item. Furthermore, beginning instruction can be summed up in the phrase, "Teach, reteach, and then teach it again." Rarely will there be a class of beginners that understand and can correctly play an instrument the first time, so plan to review everything you introduce.

1. Breathing
2. Posture
3. Opening the case/parts of the instrument/care of the instrument
4. Embouchure (using thumb)
5. Mouthpiece/barrel assembly
6. Embouchure round 2 (on mouthpiece and barrel)/first sounds
7. Introduce note symbols (rhythmic)
8. Proper hand position/how to hold the instrument
9. Long tones on mouthpiece/barrel
10. Finger exercises
11. Note shapes/releases

Clarinet

12. Counting quarter note rhythms
13. Articulation (unmetered and metered)
14. Mouthpiece/barrel (concert F-sharp) to full instrument sounds
15. E, D, and C (possibly B-flat for stability) on the instrument
16. Embouchure round 3 (mouthpiece/barrel triple check the tone and pitch—still F-sharp)
17. Learn rote songs (mi-re-do)
18. Counting quarter/half/whole note rhythms
19. The staff and reading E, D, and C (include singering)
20. G (resonance fingering/right hand down) and F on the instrument
21. Reading G, F, E, D, C (including singing)
22. Begin method book work
23. Add B-flat, A, and low G
24. Reading/sight-reading in the method book (add fingerings as needed)
25. B (both fingerings), F-sharp (both fingerings), C-sharp
26. Check mouthpiece/barrel pitch (concert F-sharp)
27. Scales using tetra chords
28. More reading and technical finger passages
29. Check embouchure by pressing register key, make necessary embouchure adjustments
30. Register slurs
31. Two octave major scales, minor scales, further technique exercises

TROUBLESHOOTING CLARINET

Problem	Possible Causes	Possible Solutions
Small/Weak Tone	⊙ Lack of wind support ⊙ Biting/embouchure too tight ⊙ Too little mouthpiece in mouth ⊙ Tight throat/tongue too high ⊙ Reed is too soft (only combined with poor wind)	⊙ Use more wind support ⊙ Decrease pressure with lower jaw or lower lip ⊙ Take more mouthpiece in mouth ⊙ Relax the throat/drop the lower tongue ⊙ Harder reed (only combined with poor wind)
Unfocused Tone	⊙ Poor reed ⊙ Bottom lip support ⊙ Mouthpiece placed incorrectly ⊙ Embouchure too loose overall ⊙ Unfocused wind stream	⊙ Check reed for chipping/warping or unevenness in tip/heart. Reed strength may be too hard/soft ⊙ Energize bottom lip more or place more bottom lip over teeth ⊙ Check that mouthpiece is centered and at the correct angle ⊙ Energize the lips evenly around the mouthpiece/reed ⊙ Blow wind to the tip opening
Weak, Fuzzy Tone	⊙ Reed too hard ⊙ Bottom lip too far inside mouth	⊙ Switch to a softer reed ⊙ Readjust bottom lip
Bright, Edgy, Reedy Tone	⊙ Reed too soft ⊙ Bottom lip not covering enough of teeth ⊙ Too much mouthpiece in mouth ⊙ Poor reed/mouthpiece combination ⊙ Overblowing	⊙ Switch to a harder reed ⊙ Readjust bottom lip ⊙ Take less mouthpiece in mouth ⊙ Reevaluate the match between reed and mouthpieces ⊙ Control wind

Clarinet

Throat Tone Quality	• Wind support lacking • Poor tongue position • Lack of embouchure energy	• Increase wind support • Be sure tongue is slightly arched • Energize the embouchure
Whistle Sounds	• Leaking corners • Fatigue	• Have students energize corners more • Provide a small break
Squeaks	• Fingers not covering holes • Reed is dry • Poor reed • Inconsistent embouchure • Too much mouthpiece in mouth • Accidental venting • Leaks in instrument • Broken/poorly made mouthpiece	• Cover holes completely • Wet reed • Check reed for chipping/warping or unevenness in tip/heart • Practice mouthpiece and barrel to stabilize F-sharp, long tones on instrument • Take less mouthpiece in mouth • Do not accidentally touch any non-essential keys • Have instrument repaired • Replace mouthpiece
Poor High Note Response	• Reed too soft • Biting • Overblowing	• Switch to harder reed • Relax jaw • Control wind
Poor Low Note Response	• Reed too hard • Leaks • Lack of wind support • Biting	• Switch to softer reed • Check instrument • Increase wind support or speed • Relax jaw
Scoop/Dip Sound	• Too much movement (jaw/tongue) • Embouchure not set	• Jaw movement is unnecessary for clarinet/use the tip of the tongue • Breath through the corners and set the lower embouchure before the attack

Clarinet

Heavy Articulation	⦿ Too much tongue pressure on reed ⦿ Too much wind pressure behind tongue ⦿ Tongue touches too low on reed	⦿ Use less tongue pressure/only use the tip tongue ⦿ Less intense wind pressure ⦿ Move the contact point higher on the reed
Flat Pitch	⦿ Barrel pulled out too far ⦿ Loose embouchure ⦿ Low tongue position/voicing ⦿ Overblowing ⦿ Incorrect instrument angle/chin ⦿ Reed is too soft ⦿ Poor mouthpiece	⦿ Push in barrel ⦿ Energize embouchure ⦿ Raise tongue ⦿ Control wind ⦿ Reset instrument angle closer to body/lift up chin ⦿ Switch to harder reed ⦿ Replace mouthpiece
Sharp Pitch	⦿ Barrel pushed in too far ⦿ Biting ⦿ Lack of wind support ⦿ Incorrect instrument angle/chin ⦿ Reed is too hard ⦿ Poor mouthpiece	⦿ Pull barrel ⦿ Relax jaw pressure ⦿ Increase wind support ⦿ Reset instrument angle further away from body/lower chin ⦿ Switch to a softer reed ⦿ Replace mouthpiece

CLARINET FINGERINGS

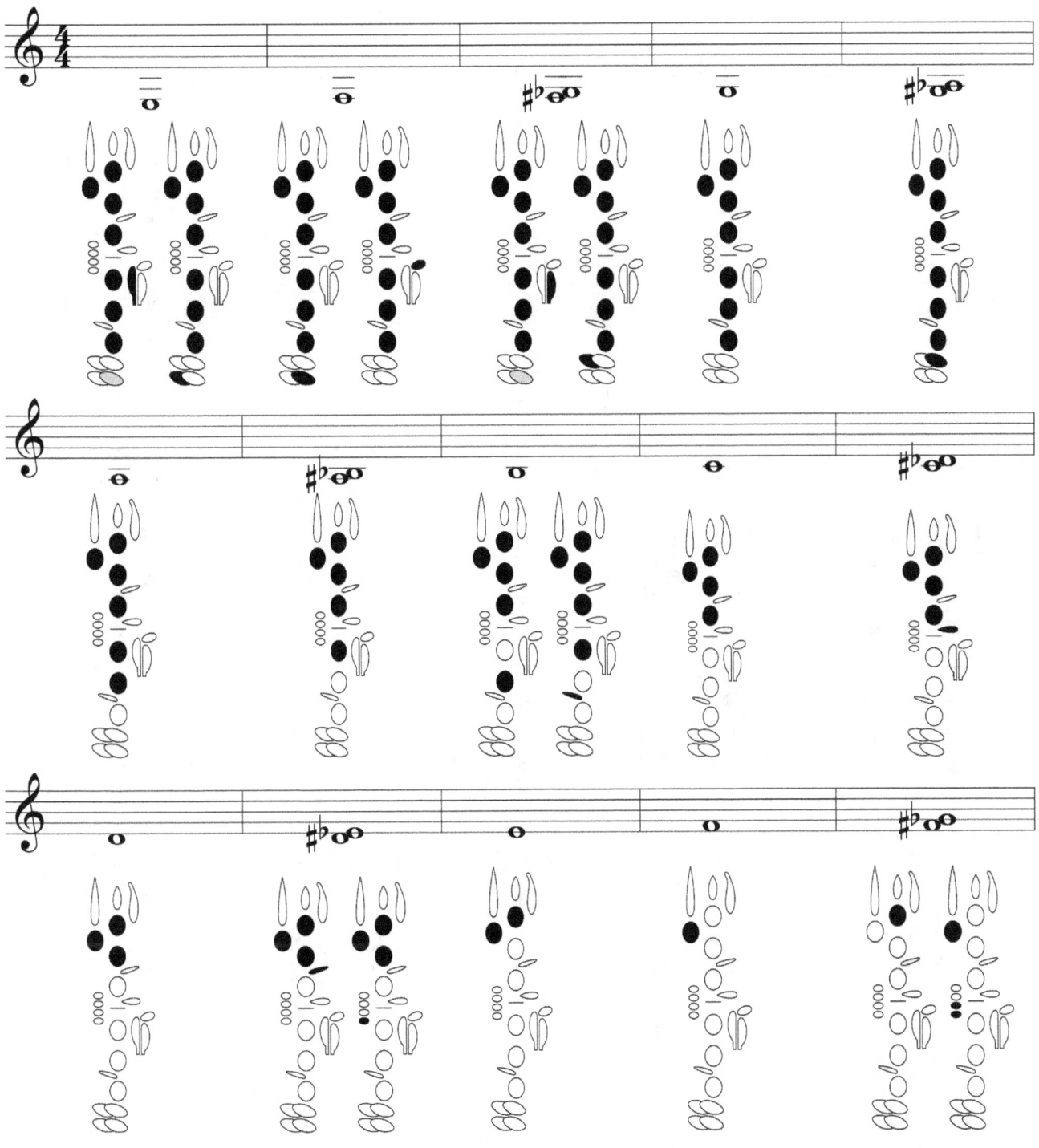

CLARINET FINGERINGS

2

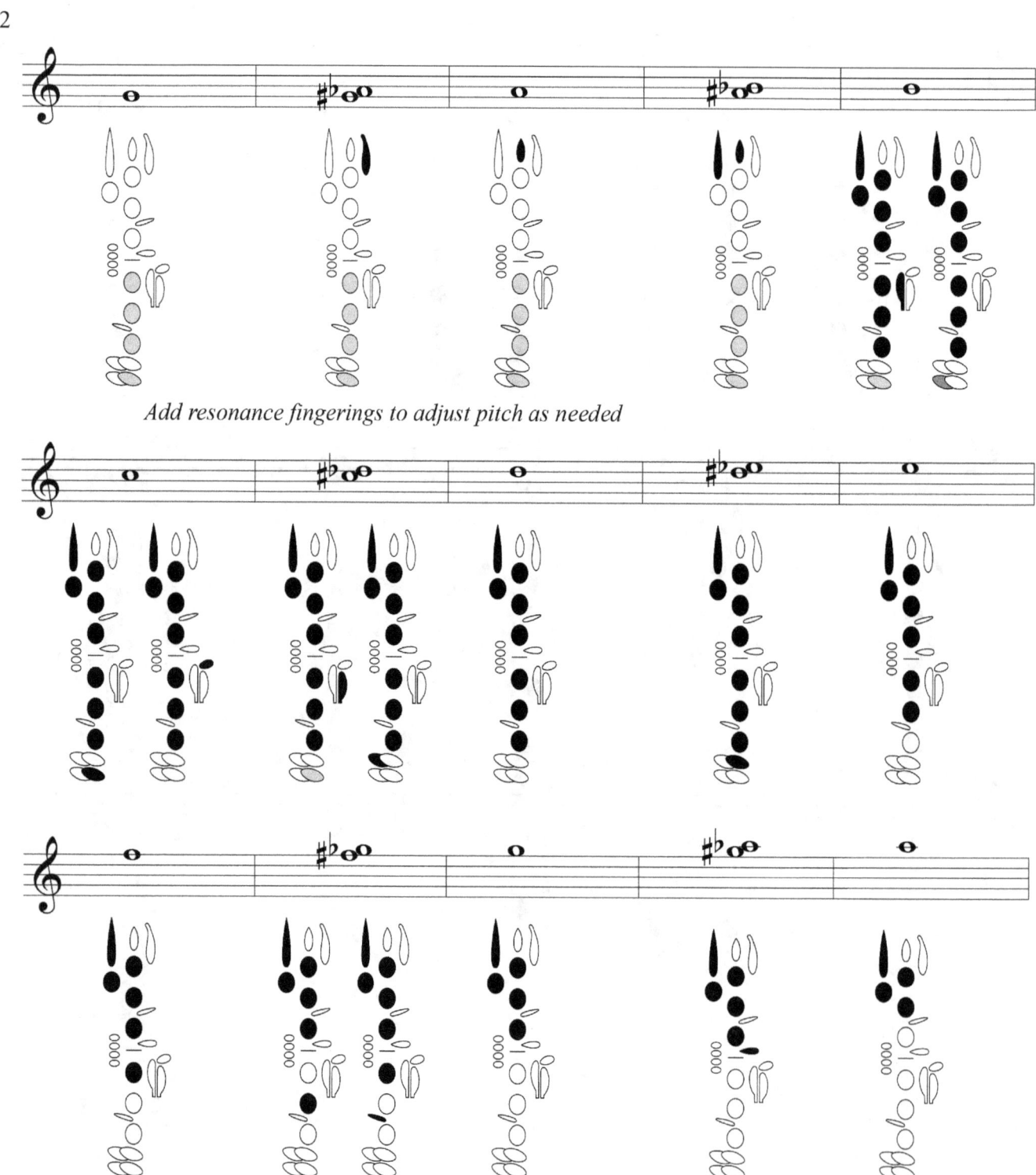

Add resonance fingerings to adjust pitch as needed

148

CLARINET FINGERINGS

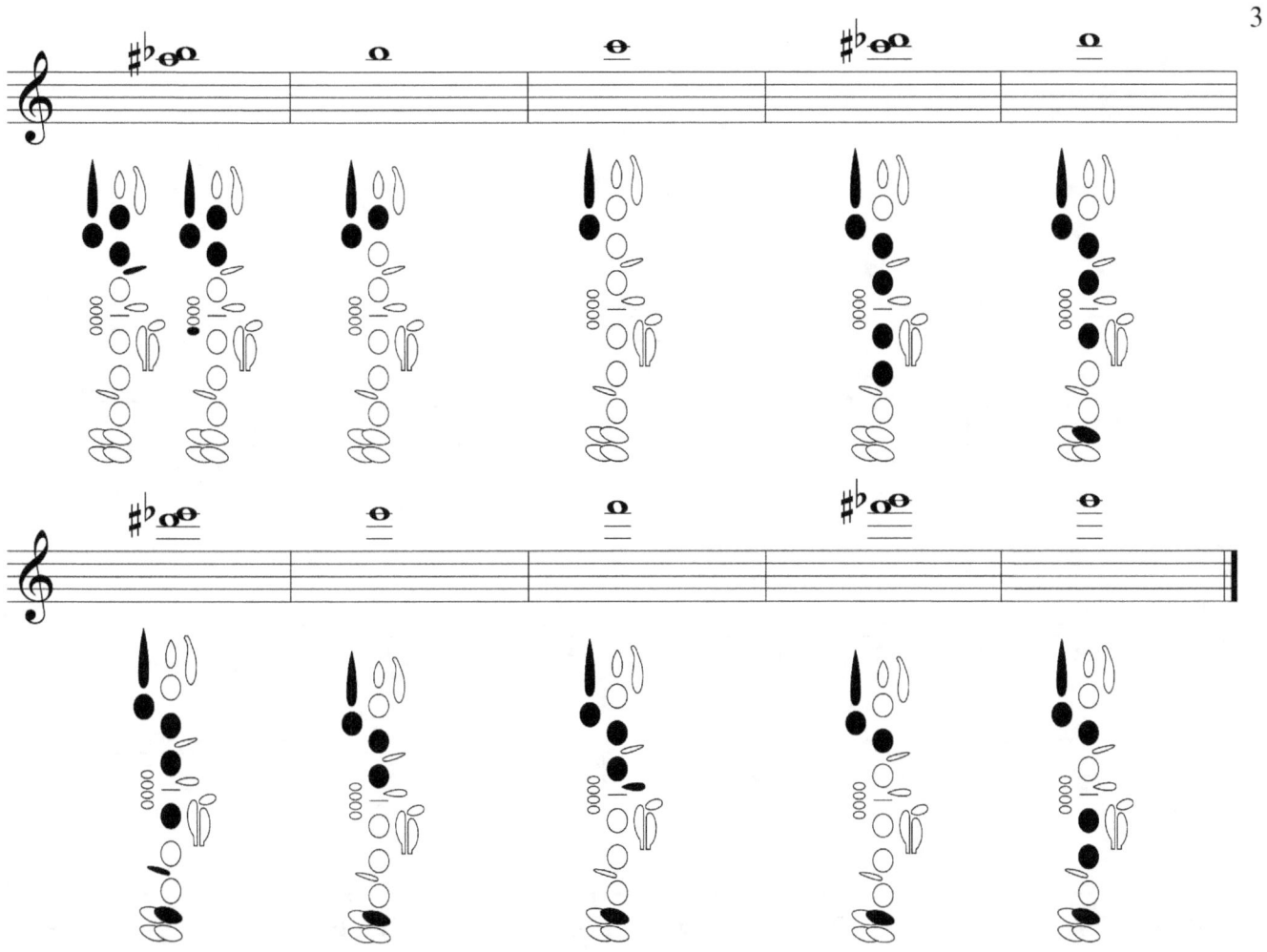

CLARINET SUPPLEMENTAL EXERCISES

CLARINET SUPPLEMENTAL EXERCISES

CLARINET SUPPLEMENTAL EXERCISES

CLARINET SUPPLEMENTAL EXERCISES

CLARINET SUPPLEMENTAL EXERCISES

CLARINET SUPPLEMENTAL EXERCISES

SAXOPHONE

07

Saxophone

Unlike many of the instruments found in band, the saxophone has a definitive inventor: Adolf Sax. Invented by Sax in 1846, saxophones are a versatile family of instruments capable of a wide range of tone qualities and the four main saxophones found in band (soprano, alto, tenor, and baritone) have remained largely unchanged since their original development. Some of the other saxophones, such as melody or bass saxes, have certain drawbacks like less stable intonation or abnormal size, and are generally excluded from most ensembles. The primary saxophones are transposing instruments in alternating keys. Therefore, alto (Figure S-1) and bari (Figure S-2) saxes are both E-flat instruments, with alto sounding a 6th lower than written and bari sounding a 14th (octave + major 6th) lower than written.

Alto

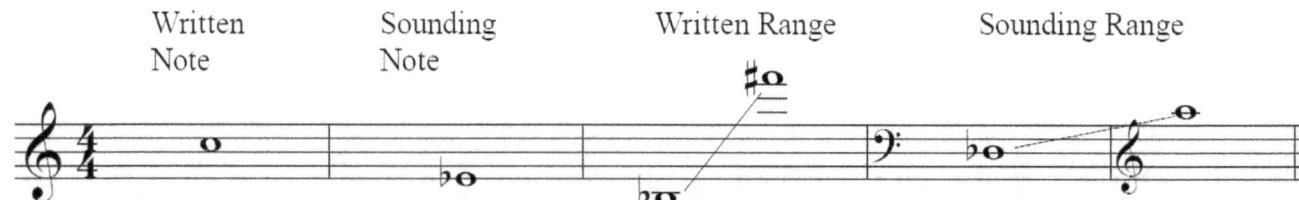

Figure S-1 Alto Range

Baritone

Figure S-2 Bari Range

Soprano (Figure S-3) and tenor (Figure S-4) saxes are both B-flat instruments, with soprano sounding a 2nd lower and tenor sounding a 9th lower than written.

Soprano

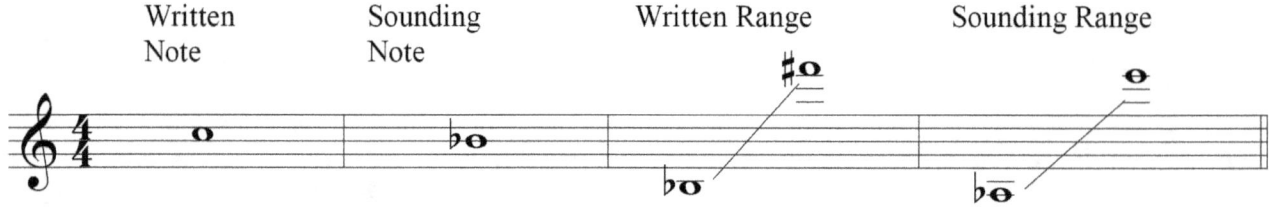

Figure S-3 Soprano Range

Saxophone

Tenor

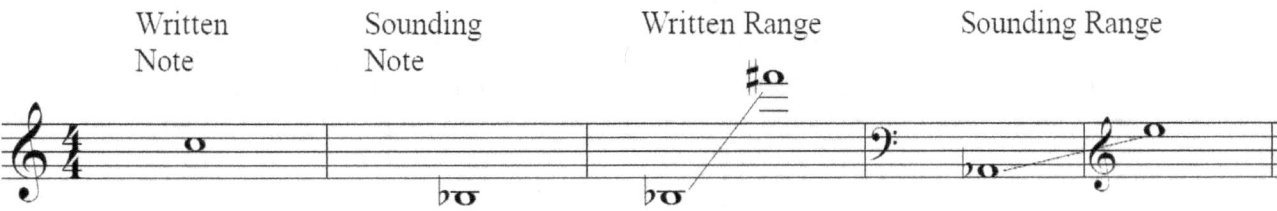

Figure S-4 Tenor Range

Of the woodwinds, saxophone is by far the easiest when it comes to basic tone production, yet one of the more difficult instruments on which to produce quality, characteristic sounds. This is due, in large part, to the forgiving nature of the instrument—saxophones will produce a sound with a wide variety of embouchures and wind uses, just not the sound directors may want in their ensembles. Beginners should master the standard notes of the instrument by the end of their first year. Altissimo extended techniques for notes above the written F6 require the use of separate fingerings and voicing adjustments. The beginner, intermediate, and advanced ranges below (Figure S-5) are all written ranges and apply to all members of the saxophone family.

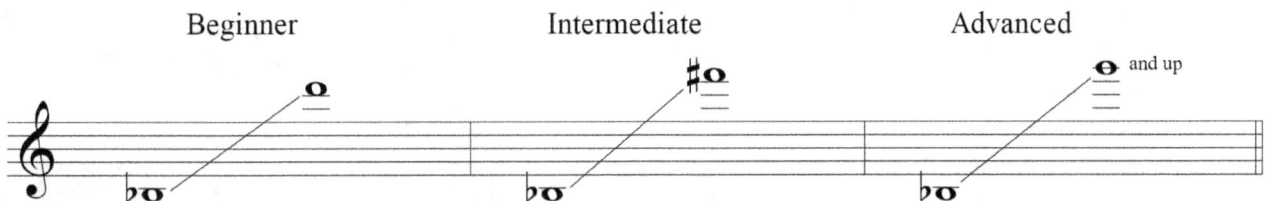

Figure S-5 Sax Skill Ranges

The majority of this section will focus on the E-flat alto saxophone, as that is the instrument most commonly taught to beginners.

INSTRUMENT SELECTION

Similar to the clarinet, begin the instrument selection process by examining student fingers. Specifically, look at finger length in Fingers 1, 2, Left Pinky, and Right Pinky. The first two fingers on the left hand need to reach around the palm keys and press the B and C keys while keeping their natural curve. The pinkies have multiple keys that they must be able to reach and provide enough strength to depress. Check the Left Pinky to see if students can reasonably reach the B and B-flat keys; on the Right Pinky, students should be able to reach the low C key.

Front teeth, also like clarinet, should ideally be even to allow for proper reed/mouthpiece contact; missing top front teeth can also impede student progress on the instrument. Look for students that have their front teeth (top and bottom) in alignment from both a teeth and jaw (overbite/underbite) perspective. It is worth noting that slight deviations are fine; students can adjust their jaws to bring teeth into alignment provided that the overbite/underbite isn't severe. Students with thick and thin lips can learn to play sax well, and lip shape is not a significant factor to tone production on the saxophone.

Finally, the weight of the instrument is a concern when working with young students. Saxophones were designed to rest largely on the neck strap or harness and trying to support the instrument with the right thumb can lead to physical injury. Students should be able to bear the weight of the instrument on their shoulders and neck. During instrument selection, I try to give the students a sense for the weight of the instrument by attaching the neck strap and placing it over their heads before slowly letting the weight rest on their neck. In some cases, the student has decided then and there that sax is not for them (which saves everyone some future headaches).

EQUIPMENT

In some band director positions, you will have the ability to influence the equipment your students procure for band class, which can be daunting on your secondary instruments. Below are some suggestions for future reference that may change due to model updates and manufacturer quality. Additionally, do not hesitate to ask other band directors or private instructors for their recommendations. This list is simply a suggestion; good players can produce great sounds on a variety of equipment and need to find the right fit for their own bodies and situations.

Figure S-6 Sax Parts

Saxophone

01 Instrument
Yamaha YAS-26, Buffett Alto 8101 (or any 100 series), Selmer AS 500

02 Mouthpieces
Selmer C*, C**, Rousseau 4R, Vandoren AL3

03 Ligature
Rovner Dark, BG L14/L14SR

04 Reeds
D'Addario Reserve Classic, Vandoren

ASSEMBLY

Saxophones are the easiest of all the woodwinds to assemble properly, though there are still important steps and considerations to avoid unnecessary, and frequent, damage. Before putting the instrument together, be sure to address opening the case, naming the parts of the instrument, and handling reeds. To assemble the entire instrument, have students begin by placing their neck strap over their head before removing the end plug from the body of the instrument. Next, students should pick up the body with both hands and attach the neck strap to the ring in the back of the saxophone. Never handle the saxophone by the neck, both the octave key and the neck itself can be bent, which prevents the instrument from working. Also, be **certain** that the neck strap is securely attached to the instrument (ones that clip/secure are better when possible.

Following the secure attachment of the neck strap, loosen the neck screw and slide in the neck, being extremely careful not to handle the octave key. Of all the possible damage during assembly, bent octave keys are by far the most common. Students should be careful where they grip the neck to avoid twisting or bending the octave key (either up by the cork or down on the bottom of the neck). Before tightening the neck screw, properly align the neck by adjusting the neck so that the bridge and the octave key are in contact, and the octave key rests closed. Many models of sax have a line on the underside of the neck that students can use as a guide to help align the bridge key. Keep in mind that, depending on playing position, this line may not exactly align with the bridge key.

Saxophone

  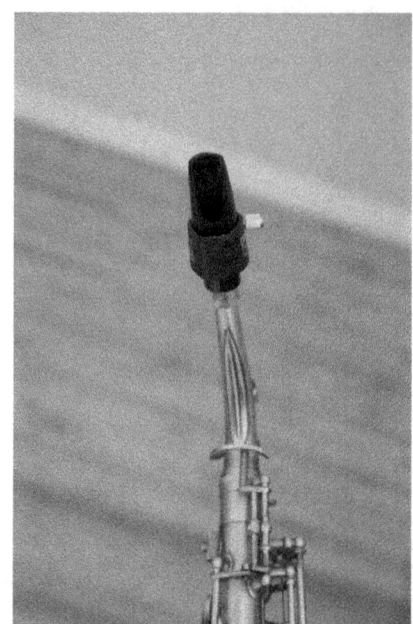

Figure S-7 Sax Assembly

Next, place the mouthpiece on the neck with the window opening downward. Students should properly grease neck corks prior to assembling the mouthpiece and take care to hold the neck just behind the cork and not on the octave key or down by the instrument body. Finally, place the ligature and then reed onto the mouthpiece.

TONE PRODUCTION AND EMBOUCHURE

After wind use, embouchure is the core component of tone production, and in the case of the saxophone, the primary purpose of the embouchure is to facilitate proper reed vibration. To that end, embouchure cannot overcome a poor reed/mouthpiece/ligature quality or combination. Regularly check student reeds for quality (warping, chipping, etc.).

The saxophone shares several embouchure and tone production traits in common with clarinet; however, there are a few key differences. Sax embouchures involve lip support for the reed/mouthpiece, and the lower lips support the reed without biting, both similar to clarinet. The angle that the mouthpiece enters the mouth, the reed/mouthpiece length (and therefore amount inside the mouth), and the position of the tongue all lead to significant differences between saxophone and clarinet tone production. Students should place their mouthpiece so that the bottom lip supports the reed slightly forward of where the reed splits from the facing. Slide a piece of paper between the reed and the mouthpiece to get a visual for where the reed and the mouthpiece separate—this will be different for different mouthpieces. Another way to estimate teeth placement is to place the top teeth approximately halfway from the tip of the mouthpiece but more accurately at the stop point where the mouthpiece and the reed touch (see figure SR-3). If possible, help place the mouthpiece/neck for first sounds so that students can get a feel for/visual of proper placement.

Because the reed enters the mouth at a wider angle (closer to parallel with the ground), the bottom lip on sax will be softer than on clarinet. I consistently refer to bottom lip as a "squishy pillow" in the early stages of embouchure development with students to avoid biting; reeds then rest on this pillow over the bottom teeth. Next, students touch the top teeth to the top of the mouthpiece. Directors should take care to assess if students are using their top lips to cushion their top teeth and correct this bad habit as early as possible (no double lip for saxes). After placing their teeth, students seal the lips by drawing the corners in and forward, similar to the drawstring on a trash bag or backpack, which has the added benefit of placing the chin in the proper place unless the student is biting.

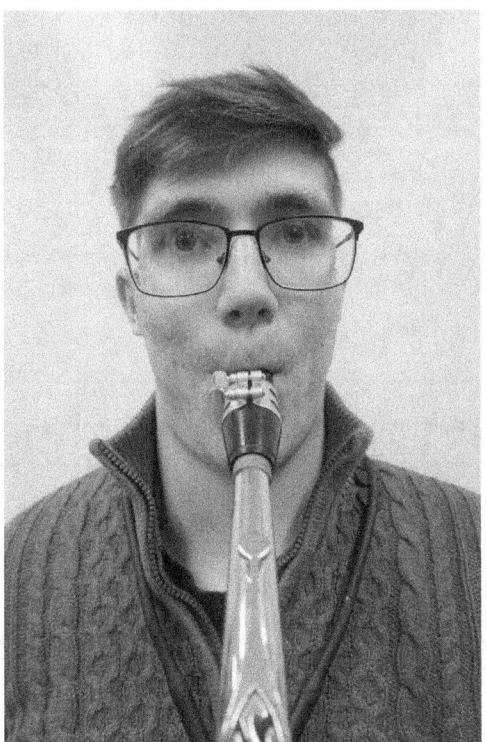 

Figure S-8 Saxophone Embouchure

Finally, the tongue should remain in a normal, relaxed position inside the mouth. Of note, while many instruments require some form of *voicing*, or changing the oral cavity during performance, this skill is necessary to produce a rich, smooth, in-tune sound on the saxophone. Voicing is largely controlled by the tongue and typically can be observed by changes in the lower jaw and throat while playing. When introducing voicing to students, I liken it to the difference between speaking normally, speaking while yawning, and baby/high-pitched speaking, as much of voicing is about opening the oral cavity, the yawning analogy is particularly helpful. To help students grasp this esoteric concept, have them play low notes (low C or below) and observe their jaws. Many young players want to lower their jaw as the principal way to get low notes to speak. While some jaw movement may be helpful, the bottom teeth should not drastically change position during low note performance. Instead, the tongue should drop and the oral cavity expands at the same time as the wind support is strengthened. Students who are voicing the low notes improperly will produce sounds above the fundamental (an important exercise for players to practice their voicing).

Once students can control their low notes (at least in terms of getting the note to speak), teachers can further build voicing (adjustments in oral cavity/throat) by having students practice harmonics. There are a few ways to do so, but I think my favorite was introduced to me by Dr. Todd Oxford and is something he calls the 2-1 exercise. For this exercise, students play a note in the middle register (for example, third-space C) and then slur to the lower note (low C). The goal is to keep the voicing the same, and therefore the sounding pitch stays the same (fingers change to low C, middle C sounds). After students have a grasp of this, students can play the low C and practice voicing the middle C. Each of these exercises can (and if directors want to do harmonics, they should) be used with multiple notes.

One final note: It is practically impossible to assess biting when performing on the mouthpiece and neck; the length provides a relatively fixed pitch (concert A-flat) regardless of jaw pressure. In other words, how far the students put the mouthpiece on the neck is the primary determiner of pitch, not embouchure. Despite this limitation, definitely start students on the mouthpiece and neck. Embouchures at the initial stages are not strong enough to handle mouthpiece performance alone, and students need to develop both muscle and wind control before they attempt to play on the mouthpiece alone. It is important, however, to check mouthpiece alone once students have a consistent embouchure to identify any excess jaw pressure or biting. An alto saxophone mouthpiece should sound a concert A, while tenor sax sounds a concert G, and baritone sax sounds concert D.

EMBOUCHURE LESSON PLAN/INSTRUCTIONAL SEQUENCE

Subject: Sax	Grade: 6	Date:

- ♪ **Concept:**
  Making a characteristic tone on the mouthpiece and neck

- ♪ **Behavioral Learning Objective:**
  Students will be able to form a characteristic embouchure and assess themselves or others regarding embouchure.

- ♪ **Standards:**
  MU:Pr5.3.E.5a/MU:Pr6.1.E.5a (National Standards example) or TEKS 117.208.C.3.B (State Standards example)

Vocabulary:
Embouchure, energize

Materials:
Mouthpiece, neck, reed, ligature

Time:
10–15 minutes

Saxophone

> **Assessment**
>
> Evaluate embouchure by comparing to an ideal image of sax embouchure, you cannot rely on mouthpiece/neck pitch for jaw pressure.

Procedures

1. Students draw their bottom lip slightly over their bottom teeth to create a "squishy pillow" where the colored part of the lip is still visible.
2. Students place their index finger on their bottom lip (index fingers general mimic the proper angle better than thumbs), being careful to avoid rolling their lip further into their mouth.
3. Students wiggle their finger to feel their teeth through the bottom lip.
4. Students close their top teeth to their fingernail.
5. Students seal their lips around their thumb, moving their corners in and slightly forward around their finger.
6. Assemble the mouthpiece/reed and neck (or mouthpiece alone if students have already demonstrated mastery with mouthpiece and neck).
7. (Optional) place mouthpiece and neck into students mouths, have them seal and blow.
8. Teacher shows students bottom lip placement on reed.
9. Students place mouthpiece and neck into mouth, seal lips, and blow wind.
10. (Optional) students remove mouthpiece from neck, place mouthpiece in mouth, seal lips, and blow wind (alto pitch = A, tenor pitch = G, bari pitch = D)

ARTICULATION

Like all wind instruments, proper wind support is necessary for correct articulation. Only the tip of the tongue is used to articulate, and the tongue acts as a release valve for the wind at the start of a note. Saxophone, like clarinet, uses the tip of the top of the tongue to touch the tip of the bottom of the reed. I use this tongue twister with my students, and we turn it into a chant that helps them remember the ideal tongue-to-reed connection when heavy tongues creep into their performance. To clarify, the bottom of the reed is the shaved side that rests on the bottom lip. Excessive tongue pressure against the reed or too much tongue/reed contact will lead to hard, aggressive attacks. Furthermore, only the tip of the tongue moves during articulation. Beginners are prone to disproportionate tongue movements or moving their jaws as they articulate.

There is some debate about using syllables to teach articulation, particularly with woodwinds. While I do not often do so, I can see the merit in a syllabic approach with one caveat: different instruments need different syllables. For sax, a doo syllable will still produce a clear start while avoiding heavy, slapping sounds. If I were to

Saxophone

use a syllable, it would be doo (particularly on the recommendation of trusted teachers) or too.

Always begin articulation instruction with connected wind and unmetered tongue movement. This allows students to concentrate on using the tip of the tongue while maintaining wind and embouchure. Remember; every time you add a new performance element or skill, students tend to struggle to maintain proficiency in the previously learned skills. After introducing the tongue motion and placement, move to metered articulation exercises.

ARTICULATION LESSON PLAN/INSTRUCTIONAL SEQUENCE

Subject: Sax   **Grade:** 6   **Date:**

- ♪ **Concept:**
  Articulating correctly on a variety of rhythms

- ♪ **Behavioral Learning Objective:**
  Students will be able to perform articulated notes in a variety of rhythms while maintaining proper embouchure.

- ♪ **Standards:**
  MU:Pr5.3.E.5a/MU:Pr6.1.E.5a/ MU:Pr4.2.E.5a (National Standards example) or TEKS 117.208.C.3.B (State Standards example)

Vocabulary:
Articulation, tonguing, quarter notes, stability, legato

Materials:
Mouthpiece, neck, reed, ligature, white/chalk board, entire instrument (optional)

Time:
15–20 minutes

Procedures

1. Students play mouthpiece and neck.
2. Students touch top of the tip of the tongue to the bottom of the tip of the reed.
3. (Optional) Teacher models articulation sound for students.
4. Students blow wind and move their tongue without the mouthpiece and neck – teacher assesses wind consistency.
5. Teacher models unmetered articulation for students.
6. Students blow wind and move their tongue with proper embouchure on mouthpiece and neck – unmetered practice.
7. Teacher models metered quarter notes – full value.
8. Students perform quarter notes on mouthpiece and neck (be sure to watch/listen for students who are cheating by using a breath or "who" start).
9. Students articulate notes on the entire instrument.

(This page left intentionally blank)

PLAYING POSITION

There are two separate playing positions for the alto sax when the performer is seated: instrument to the side and instrument in the middle (Figure S-9). Most beginners should start with the instrument body on their right side, due to student height. The mouthpiece must be adjusted so that it enters the mouth parallel to the lips without tilting the head left/right, and students should take care not to let the body of the instrument drop too far back or push too far forward along their right leg. Neck strap placement is key to instrument angle, and directors should stress to their students that the instrument should naturally come to the face/lips instead of moving any portion of their body to the instrument. The head and chin should remain neutral and the saxophone, with proper neck strap adjustment, will pivot directly to the lips. Due to the nature of weight displacement (primarily the neck strap), young saxophonists are prone to developing posture problems early.

Figure S-9 Saxophone Playing Position

The second playing position for alto sax is for the body of the instrument to be in the middle, aligned with the student's spine. Playing in this position will make students less prone to poor posture habits, but until the student's torso is long enough, holding the instrument this way greatly affects right hand position. Therefore, middle position should only be used by students of sufficient height; once the student is tall enough, this is by far the preferred position among more advanced performers because it allows for better breathing. Additionally, in standing position, all alto saxes should be held in the middle/aligned with the spine.

Finger position is crucial in developing technique; however, inexperienced teachers may overlook bad habits when focusing on tone production. Fingers should keep a natural curve, with the finger pads touching the pearls of the keys (Figure S-10). Left thumb position is also important for octave changes. Students should rest their left thumb on the thumb rest near the first knuckle at a 2 o'clock position so that the thumb can rock to the octave key without needing to slide or lift away from the instrument. Lastly, students must keep pinkies curved and in a position that allows them to slide across the rollers to multiple keys. This may be challenging for beginners, as they often lift their pinkies far from the instrument without noticing. Gently remind beginners to keep all of their fingers close or in contact with the instrument at all times while playing.

Figure S-10 Saxophone Hand Position

INTONATION

Intonation on saxophone is primarily created by wind support, mouthpiece/reed, and embouchure. Without these things, tuning the instrument by mechanical means is extremely difficult. With beginners, greater time and focus on the sources of intonation problems will better serve student performance. The primary method of adjusting mechanical intonation on the saxophone is the mouthpiece position on the neck; proper mouthpiece placement on the neck is normally around two thirds of the way on the neck. Pulling the mouthpiece out will lower the pitch, while pushing in will raise the pitch.

The saxophone can be tuned using the following notes (S-11):

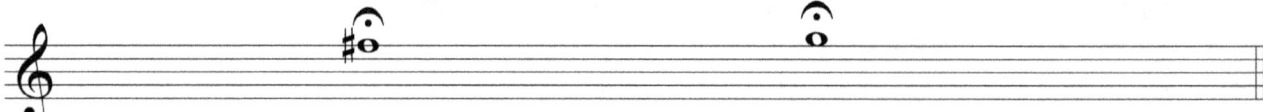

Figure S-11 Saxophone Tuning Notes

Additionally, the following notes show some of the more egregious intonation challenges on the alto sax (S-12):

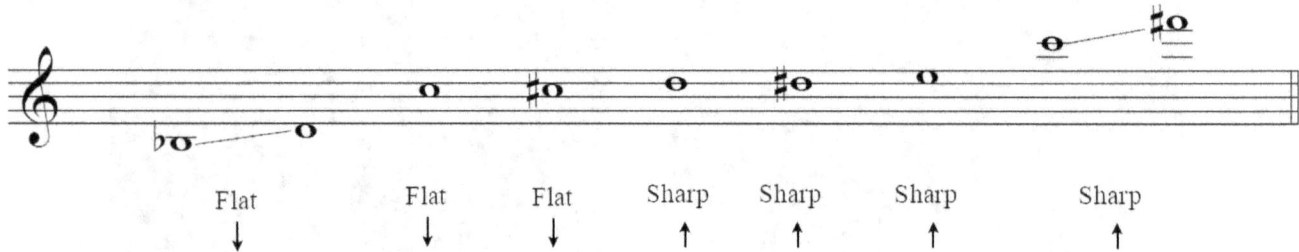

Figure S-12 Saxophone Intonation Concerns

Several aspects of the mouthpiece/reed affect intonation. Reeds that are too hard tend to play sharp, while those that are too soft tend to play flat. Furthermore, the amount of mouthpiece in the mouth and playing position angle can also influence tuning. Too large a playing angle (bell too far from body) leads to flat sounds and too small a playing angle (bell too close to the body or back by the back pockets) plays sharp. Mouthpieces should enter the mouth at a marginally upward angle and students should adjust next straps so that the instrument naturally pivots to this position in their mouth. Finally, mouthpieces with a closed facing may tend to be sharper than those with open facings.

All wind instruments have intonation considerations when changing dynamics. During crescendos, the sax tends to drift flat. Conversely, the sax is inclined to play sharp during decrescendos. Players can use their embouchures or voicing to offset both tendencies, provided they have solid embouchure control and are aware of the proclivities of the instrument.

Saxophone

VIBRATO

Vibrato on the saxophone is a component of quality tone, and players largely create vibrato through jaw movement. To teach vibrato to young saxophonists, focus on the pitch changes and direct students to make small, smooth undulations with their jaw. If students have mastered the appropriate jaw pressure (as checked by the mouthpiece pitch), the small adjustments to alter pitch above and below center should be easy. I typically ask students to make small, circular motions with their jaw to raise and lower the pitch slightly by changing the jaw pressure on the vibrating reed. While the motions are not exactly circular, I have found that giving that descriptor helps to smooth/even out the motion early in the process. Other pedagogues use the syllable "yew" to describe the jaw motion (have students say "yew-yew-yew"), which also works well. Additionally, I recommend teaching vibrato unmetered and tasking students with adjusting the speed at varying levels and times. If directors decide to teach vibrato with metric pulses, vary the subdivision regularly.

THE SAXOPHONE FAMILY

It is common for more advanced players to tackle the four main saxophones (soprano, alto, tenor, and baritone) during their musical career. When starting beginners on saxophone, I suggest using alto exclusively, due to instrument size and ease of embouchure control compared to the other instruments in the family. Fortunately, the fingerings are identical across all saxophones, as are the fundamentals of embouchure and tone production. All saxophones are transposing instruments (as mentioned earlier) and the majority used in modern settings are in either B-flat or Eb.

The B-flat soprano saxophone is the smallest, and therefore highest pitched, of the four main instruments and comes in two body shapes: curved and straight. Both sound in the same range and are capable of fast, technical passages; however, the curved model typically has more intonation problems. Controlling tone and intonation on the soprano can pose quite a challenge to young players, due to the physical nature of the instrument (i.e., mouthpiece/reed size, amount of mouthpiece placed in mouth) combined with the high frequency of produced sounds. Therefore, players will need to control their embouchure, voicing, and wind to center the tone and make frequent intonation adjustments. I'd like to specifically point out that corner strength is essential to control soprano tone, and students will need time to build said strength if they are new

to the instrument. Similar to horn, students who are able to audiate well are able to learn the necessary adjustments with greater ease. In general, the soprano should be played by students who have already demonstrated success on another saxophone.

The B-flat tenor saxophone is a staple of various jazz and popular music over the course of the twentieth century. It sounds lower than the alto and is larger (both in length and in general size) than either the soprano or alto, which directors should take into consideration with younger players. Controlling low notes on the tenor is more difficult than alto, and students will need to adjust their embouchure and voicings slightly to accommodate for the larger mouthpiece/reed and longer instrument. To that end, students also need to take slightly more mouthpiece in their mouth in order to make the appropriate sound. Adjustment for intonation, while similar to the alto, requires that students lightly exaggerate any physical motions when compared to what they would do on the alto.

The E-flat baritone (or bari) sax is the largest of the commonly used saxophones in band and size is the biggest (pun fully intended) thing to consider when switching a student to bari. Simply assembling the instrument can prove a Herculean task to a small student, and real physical harm can happen to those who play the instrument who are unable to support the weight. When possible, I recommend students use a harness instead of a neck strap to distribute the weight more efficiently/evenly. Furthermore, bari saxes require a considerable amount of wind (on par with some euphoniums or tubas, in my opinion) to play well. Notes in the extreme ranges tend to have more egregious intonation problems on baritone sax compared to the other three saxes. Finally, the small neck poses a risk, as players struggling with the unwieldy body have been known to bend or crush the neck accidentally. Encourage your students to either assemble the entire instrument at their case or, if they are strong enough, to assemble the neck/mouthpiece and carry it in one hand and the body in another.

IDEAL AURAL IMAGES

1. Sigurd Rascher
2. Eugene Rousseau
3. Kenneth Tse
4. Claude Delangle
5. Timothy Mcallister
6. Todd Oxford
7. Otis Murphy
8. Arno Bornkamp
9. Valentine Michaud
10. Amy Dickson

Saxophone

SELECTED BEGINNER RESOURCES

The Eugene Rousseau Saxophone Method Book 1— by Rousseau, published by Kjos

Selected Studies for Saxophone — by Voxman, published by Rubank

Selected Duets for Saxophone — by Voxman, published by Rubank

Universal Method for Saxophone — by DeVille, published by Allegro Editions

Rubank Elementary Method— by Hovey, published by Hal Leonard

PRACTICAL TIPS

Assembly

- Always open the case on the floor.
- Beginners should avoid handling the octave key itself whenever possible; this is the most commonly damaged part of the saxophone.
- Students should always hold the sax with at least one hand.
    - Assume all neck straps are two seconds away from breaking.
    - Don't trust neck straps to handle the swinging and swaying of the instrument while students move around, either.
- Loosen the screw at the top of the body before making any adjustment to the neck position, especially taking it off/putting it on—the metal will get shaved off and the neck will no longer stay in one position if students skip this step.
- Reeds are last on and first off.
- Ligature screws almost always are turned by the right hand; doublecheck ligatures as part of fixing bad tones.
- Ligatures need to go down far enough on the mouthpiece to be past the line of bark on the reed.
    - Ligatures are conical, so make sure that it can slide far enough down the mouthpiece.
- Stop tightening screws when you feel resistance—overtightening is a thing and impacts sound/reed vibration.

- Cork grease must be rubbed into new corks. (You can tell by the color—light brown is less greased.)
  - Don't grease the metal at the bottom of the neck; if it is sticking clean the tenon with a damp paper towel.
- Reeds should be aligned with the tip of the mouthpiece.
  - My go-to for telling students when they are aligned is to see black at the tip when looking at the reed and see reed at the tip when looking at the top of the mouthpiece.
  - Never touch the tip of the reed to check placement (or for any other reason).
  - Reed placement can greatly impact tone, check students regularly
- Broken/chipped reeds will not consistently produce good sounds.
  - Students should rotate reeds to increase longevity.

Embouchure

- Reed vibrations create the sound; therefore bottom lip and reed quality/placement are paramount for tone production.
- Energize from the corners—like a drawstring bag.
- Start with mouthpiece and neck, but don't emphasize the A-flat pitch—that will be largely affected by mouthpiece placement instead of jaw pressure.
- Mouthpiece alone is great for assessing bottom jaw pressure, but requires strong corners before attempting.
  - Know the correct mouthpiece pitch for each type of sax (soprano - C-sharp; alto – A; tenor – G; baritone - D) to avoid giving incorrect feedback
  - Once students are strong enough in the corners, mix in mouthpiece alone to the routine, but don't use it exclusively.
- Generally, students should place approximately half of the mouthpiece into their mouth.
  - A more accurate way to check is to slide a piece of paper between the mouthpiece and the reed, where it stops is the delineation between inside the mouth and outside.
  - Too little in the mouth leads to thin, weak sounds.
  - Too much in the mouth is loud and spread.
- Tongue rests in a relaxed natural/neutral position when not voicing or articulating.

- Biting is incredibly common among young saxophonists.
    - Check the pitch on the mouthpiece alone.
    - Biting leads to sharp, pinched sounds and significant trouble getting low notes to speak.
- Dropping the jaw is **not** the universal solution to poor/unresponsive low notes.
    - Make sure the student isn't biting, then move on to wind use and voicing as likely problems.
- Spend time matching tone to ideal aural images is the best way to refine tone quality on the sax (and really most instruments).

Articulation

- Proper wind and embouchure are necessary for articulation; do not teach articulation until these are relatively well established.
- Tonguing does not stop the reed from vibrating.
- Tip of the top of the tongue touches the tip of the bottom of the reed.
    - Bottom of the reed is the side with bark and rests on the bottom lip.
- Fast tongue movements, even on slow notes.
- Let them experiment and work to match attack/articulation sounds with a model.
- Try to avoid anchor tonguing (putting the tip of the tongue against the bottom teeth and moving the middle of the tongue) when possible.
- Likewise, the tongue should never touch the roof of the mouth while articulating.
- Wind flows out when playing, in when breathing only. Articulation is more like waving a hand across an open faucet of water; the water never stops, nor should the wind.

Playing Position

- The saxophone comes to the body, never the other way around.
    - Small details in posture will depend on the individual performer.
        - Only use middle position if students' torsos are tall enough to allow for the right hand to access the keys unobstructed.
        - When using side position, the instrument will often be near the middle of the thigh; judge by how the mouthpiece enters the mouth.

- Neck straps should be positioned so that the mouthpiece naturally pivots to the correct spot on the face/mouth.
    - Side or center positions still have to have the mouthpiece in the right spot.
- Weight **does not** rest on the right thumb; it is for balance only.
- Keep fingers curved.
- The sax should never rest against the chair.
- Elbows should never touch any other part of the body.
- Left thumb should be able to pivot/rock and press the octave key without breaking contact from the thumb rest.
- Left hand fingers reach around the palm keys/left side keys.
- Watch out for shoulder tension among younger players as they get used to the weight; shoulders should be relaxed and even.

Other Tips

- Producing characteristic tone on the sax is like being Goldilocks—you have to find the thing that is just right. (Think of it as the Zen art of saxophone!)
    - The right amount of jaw pressure—too much leads to thin, pinched sound and too little leads to spread blasting.
    - The right wind support—too much leads to loud honking while too little leads to thin, fuzzy sounds.
    - The right amount of mouthpiece in the mouth—too much leads to squawking similar to overblowing, too little leads to weak sounds (or no sound at all).
    - The right strength of reed—too hard is fuzzy and quiet, while too soft is loud and edgy.
- Saxophones will make some kind of sound in most circumstances (not necessarily the sound you want). Teach students to assess themselves to improve their tones.
- Tongue position will change depending on the notes being played (known as voicing).
- Practice finger patterns to give faces a break early in the year.
- Reeds matter.
    - Reed rotations are necessary—insist on a bare minimum of three working reeds (five preferable).
    - Check reeds often. Don't assume students are on top of reed rotations, maintenance, or placement

Saxophone

during their beginner experience.

- Not all reeds that come from a box are created equal.
- Reed strength needs to match tip opening/mouthpiece shape; the wider the tip opening the softer the reed.

♪ Woodwind technique is largely making students do a large variety of technical patterns a ridiculous number of times.

♪ Intonation is complicated.

- Consistent tone is a prerequisite for effective intonation.
- Reeds matter with intonation too.
- So does everything else (embouchure, mouthpiece model/shape, ligature, tongue position, wind support, etc.).
- Mechanical adjustments of pitch happen primarily at the mouthpiece.
- Voicing can also impact intonation significantly.
- Mouthpiece shape and material can also affect tuning; jazz mouthpieces with a more open lay sometimes (depending on material) play sharper than classical mouthpieces.

♪ When you can, start everyone on the same brand/model mouthpieces.

♪ Force correct repetitions of difficult finger combinations:

- Proper uses of both B-flat fingerings
- Proper uses of both F-sharp fingerings
- Pinkies
- C/C-sharp/D
- Palm keys

♪ If embouchure and voicing are correct and low notes still don't speak easily, check reeds and also make sure nothing (reed boxes, swabs, tuners, etc.) has fallen into the bell of the instrument.

♪ Stock mouthpieces are, by and large, not effective at producing characteristic tones. Get students on quality mouthpieces made out of appropriate materials.

TROUBLESHOOTING SAXOPHONE

Problem	Possible Causes	Possible Solutions
Small/Weak Tone	⊙ Lack of wind support ⊙ Biting/embouchure too tight ⊙ Too little mouthpiece in mouth ⊙ Tight throat/tongue too high	⊙ Use more wind support ⊙ Decrease pressure with lower jaw or lower lip ⊙ Take more mouthpiece in mouth ⊙ Relax the throat/drop the tongue
Unfocused Tone	⊙ Embouchure too loose overall ⊙ Poor reed ⊙ Bottom lip support ⊙ Mouthpiece placed incorrectly ⊙ Unfocused wind stream ⊙ Wind speed	⊙ Energize the lips evenly around the mouthpiece/reed ⊙ Check reed for chips, warping, or unevenness in tip/heart. Reed strength may be too hard ⊙ Energize bottom lip more or place more bottom lip over teeth ⊙ Check that mouthpiece is centered and at the correct angle ⊙ Blow wind to the tip opening ⊙ Adjust wind speed for better tone
Weak, Fuzzy Tone	⊙ Reed too hard ⊙ Bottom lip too far inside mouth	⊙ Switch to a softer reed ⊙ Readjust bottom lip
Bright, Edgy, Reedy Tone	⊙ Reed too soft ⊙ Bottom lip not covering enough of teeth ⊙ Too much mouthpiece in mouth ⊙ Poor reed/mouthpiece combination ⊙ Overblowing ⊙ Poor reed	⊙ Switch to a harder reed ⊙ Readjust bottom lip ⊙ Take less mouthpiece in mouth ⊙ Reevaluate the match between reed and mouthpieces ⊙ Control wind ⊙ Check reed for chipping/warping

Saxophone

Loud, Spread Tone	⊙ Too much mouthpiece in mouth ⊙ Overblowing	⊙ Take less mouthpiece in mouth ⊙ Control wind speed
Thin, Pinched Ton	⊙ Biting ⊙ Reed too soft ⊙ Too little mouthpiece in mouth	⊙ Relax the jaw or embouchure ⊙ Switch to a harder reed ⊙ Take more mouthpiece into mouth
Whistle Sounds	⊙ Leaking corners ⊙ Fatigue	⊙ Have students energize corners more ⊙ Provide a small break
Gurgling Sounds	⊙ Water in a tone hole ⊙ Water in the mouthpiece/neck	⊙ Short term: Blow wind into the tone hole to remove water Long term: Swab the instrument regularly ⊙ Short term: Suck the condensation out of the reed, take off neck and shake out excess water Long term: Swab the neck/clean the mouthpiece regularly
Poor High Note Response	⊙ Reed too soft ⊙ Biting ⊙ Overblowing	⊙ Switch to harder reed ⊙ Relax jaw ⊙ Control wind
Poor Low Note Response	⊙ Reed too hard ⊙ Leaks ⊙ Lack of wind support ⊙ Biting ⊙ Voicing is too high	⊙ Switch to softer reed ⊙ Check instrument ⊙ Increase wind support or speed ⊙ Relax jaw ⊙ Lower tongue/relax throat to voice the note lower
Scoop/Dip Sound	⊙ Too much movement (jaw/tongue) ⊙ Embouchure not set	⊙ Jaw movement is unnecessary for saxophone/use the tip of the tongue ⊙ Breath through the corners and set the lower embouchure before the attack

Saxophone

Heavy Articulation	<ul><li>Too much tongue pressure on reed</li><li>Too much wind pressure behind tongue</li><li>Tongue touches too low on reed</li></ul>	<ul><li>Use less tongue pressure/only use the tip tongue</li><li>Less intense wind pressure</li><li>Move the contact point higher on the reed</li></ul>
Flat Pitch	<ul><li>Mouthpiece pulled out too far</li><li>Loose embouchure</li><li>Overblowing</li><li>Incorrect instrument angle</li><li>Chin tilted toward chest</li><li>Reed is too soft</li><li>Note is voiced too low</li></ul>	<ul><li>Push in barrel</li><li>Energize embouchure</li><li>Control wind</li><li>Reset instrument angle closer to body</li><li>Raise chin to be parallel with floor</li><li>Switch to harder reed</li><li>Raise tongue slightly for proper voicing</li></ul>
Sharp Pitch	<ul><li>Mouthpiece pushed in too far</li><li>Biting</li><li>Lack of wind support</li><li>Incorrect instrument angle</li><li>Reed is too hard</li><li>Note is voiced too high</li></ul>	<ul><li>Pull mouthpiece</li><li>Relax jaw pressure</li><li>Increase wind support</li><li>Reset instrument angle further away from body</li><li>Switch to a softer reed</li><li>Relax tongue/open throat for proper voicing</li></ul>

SAXOPHONE FINGERINGS

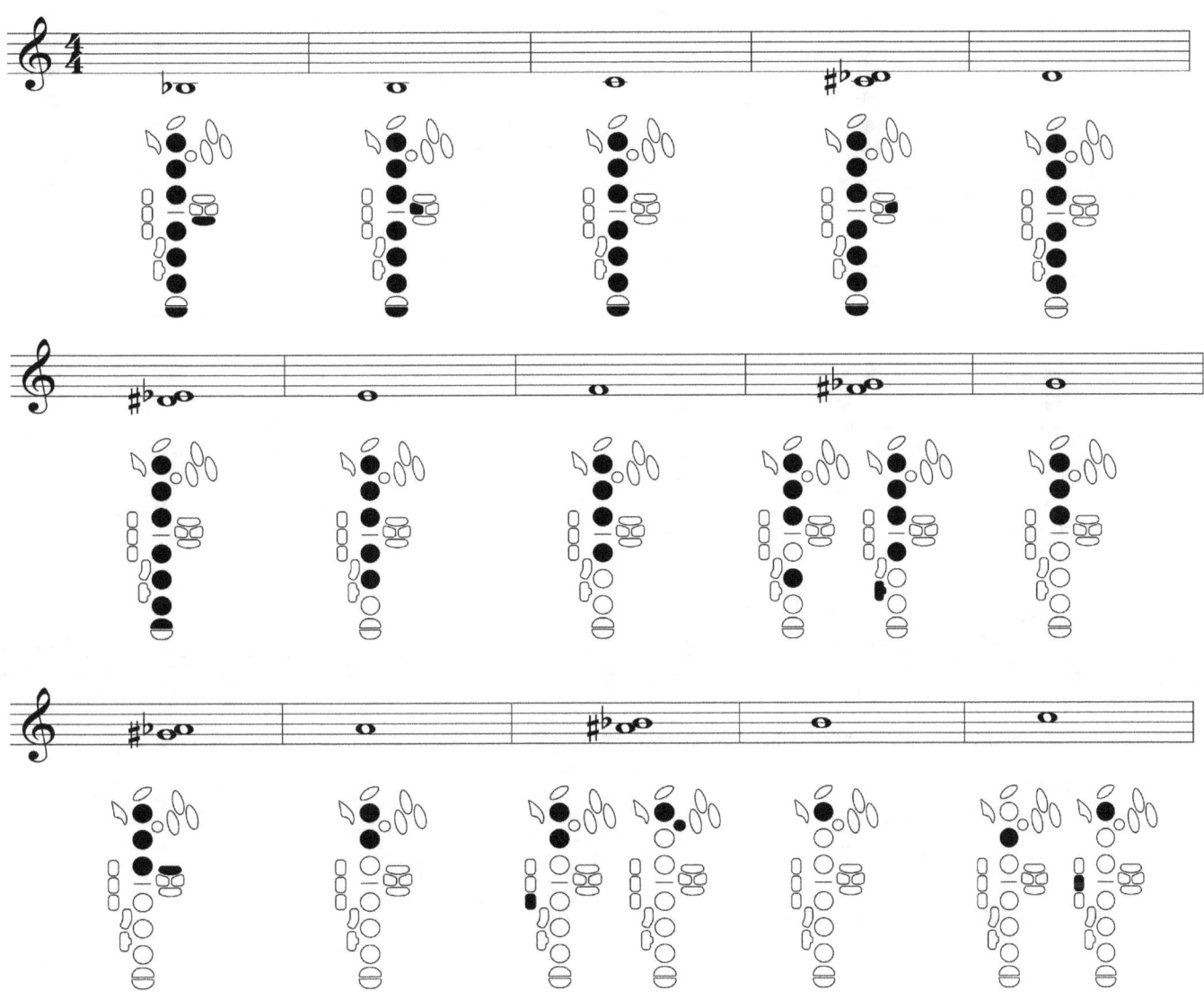

SAXOPHONE FINGERINGS

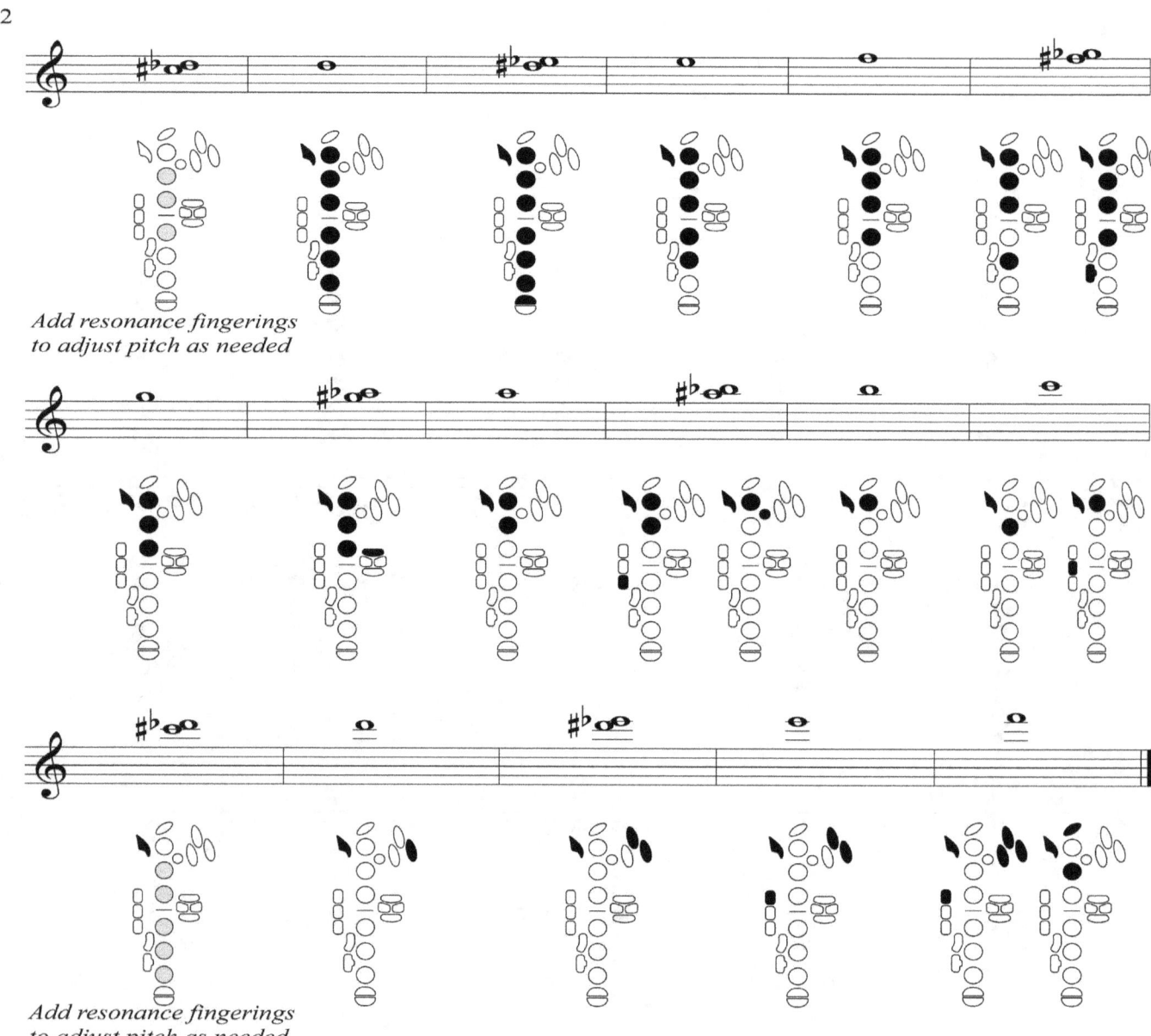

SAX SUPPLEMENTAL EXERCISES

SAX SUPPLIMENTAL EXERCISES

184

SAX SUPPLIMENTAL EXERCISES

© 2025 Agogic Pres

Agogic Press grants permission to duplicate this worksheet for non-profit, educational use only, provided each copy includes this copyright notice. Copies may not be sold or included in any materials offered for sale or for any form of profit.

SAX SUPPLEMENTAL EXERCISES

SAX SUPPLEMENTAL EXERCISES

REFERENCES

Barris, Robert, and Michael Jampole. 2008. "First Lessons on Bassoon." *Instrumentalist* 63 (4): 51.

Bayley, Jonathan. 2006. "Fundamental of Teaching Flute Vibrato." *Canadian Winds / Vents Canadiens* 5 (1): 30–32.

Brown, Jeremy S. 1999. "Improving Saxophone Intonation." *Instrumentalist* 54 (2): 36.

Brown, Peter C., Henry L. Roediger III, and Mark A. McDaniel. *Make It Stick: The Science of Successful Learning*. The Belknap Press of Harvard University Press, 2014.

Cavitt, Mary Ellen. 2012. *On Teaching Band: Notes from Eddie Green*. Hal Leonard.

Clardy, Mary Karen. 1993. *Flute Fundamentals: The Building Blocks of Technique*. European American Music Corporation.

Dietz, William. 1998. *Teaching Woodwinds: A Method and Resource Handbook for Music Educators*. Schirmer Books.

Denis, J.M., ed. 2022. *Program Notes: A Comprehensive Guide to Band Directing / Compiled and Edited by John M. Denis*. GIA Publications, Inc.

Duke, Robert A. 2005. *Intelligent Music Teaching: Essays on the Core Principles of Effective Instruction*. Austin, TX: Learning and Behavior Resources.

Ely, Mark C., and Amy E. Van Deuren. 2009. *Wind Talk for Woodwinds: A Practical Guide to Understanding and Teaching Woodwind Instruments*. Oxford University Press.

Gardner, Joshua Thomas. 2010. "Ultrasonographic Investigation of Clarinet Multiple Articulation." D.M.A., Arizona State University. **https://www.proquest.com/docview/506682827/abstract/B48D4AB6A17D4BE3PQ/1.**

Goossens, Leon, and Edwin Roxburgh. 1977. *Oboe*. Schirmer Books.

Hemke, Frederick L., and David Demsey. 2008. "First Lessons on the Saxophone." *Instrumentalist* 62 (7): 44.

Griswold, Harold Gene. 2008. *Teaching Woodwinds*. Pearson/Prentice Hall.

References

Holton, Arthur J. 1990. "Guiding Beginners on Clarinet and Saxophone." *Instrumentalist* 45 (2): 64.

Jessup, Carol A. 2014. "Clarinet Class." *School Band & Orchestra* 17 (10): 20–23.

Jones, Katherine Borst. 2012. "Teaching Fundamentals of Flute Playing." *Triad* 80 (2): 83–84.

Koster, Keith. 2010. "Revisiting Teaching Strategies for Woodwinds." *Music Educators Journal* 96 (3): 44–52. **https://doi.org/10.1177/0027432109358974**.

Louke, Phyllis Avidan. 2015. "First Lessons for the Beginning Flutist, Part2." *Flute Talk* 35 (2): 38–40.

Lulich, Steven M., Sherman Charles, and Benjamin Lulich. 2017. "The Relation between Tongue Shape and Pitch in Clarinet Playing Using Ultrasound Measurements." *The Journal of the Acoustical Society of America* 141 (3): 1759. **https://doi.org/10.1121/1.4978059**.

Miksza, Peter. 2012. "The Development of a Measure of Self-Regulated Practice Behavior for Beginning and Intermediate Instrumental Music Students." *Journal of Research in Music Education*, no. 4: 321.

Millican, J. Si. 2017. "Band Instrument Selection and Assignment: A Review of the Literature." *UPDATE: Applications of Research in Music Education* 35 (2): 46–53. **https://doi.org/10.1177/8755123315610174**.

Pino, David. 1998. *The Clarinet and Clarinet Playing*. Courier Corporation.

Rothwell, Evelyn. 1983. *Oboe Technique, (3rd ed)*. Oxford University Press.

Schuring, Martin. 2009. *Oboe Art and Method*. Oxford University Press.

Seaton, John. 2014. "The Art of Teaching Saxophone." *Instrumentalist* 69 (3): 8–12.

Sprenkle, Robert, and David Ledet. 1961. *The Art of Oboe Playing: Including Problems and Techniques of Oboe Reedmaking, (1st ed)*, Alfred Music.

Westphal, 1990, *Guide to Teaching Woodwinds (5th ed)*, W. C. Brown Company.

Winkle, Carola K. 2012. "Teaching Clarinet Fundamentals." *Instrumentalist* 67 (1): 24–30.

HETERGENEOUS WOODWIND EXERCISES

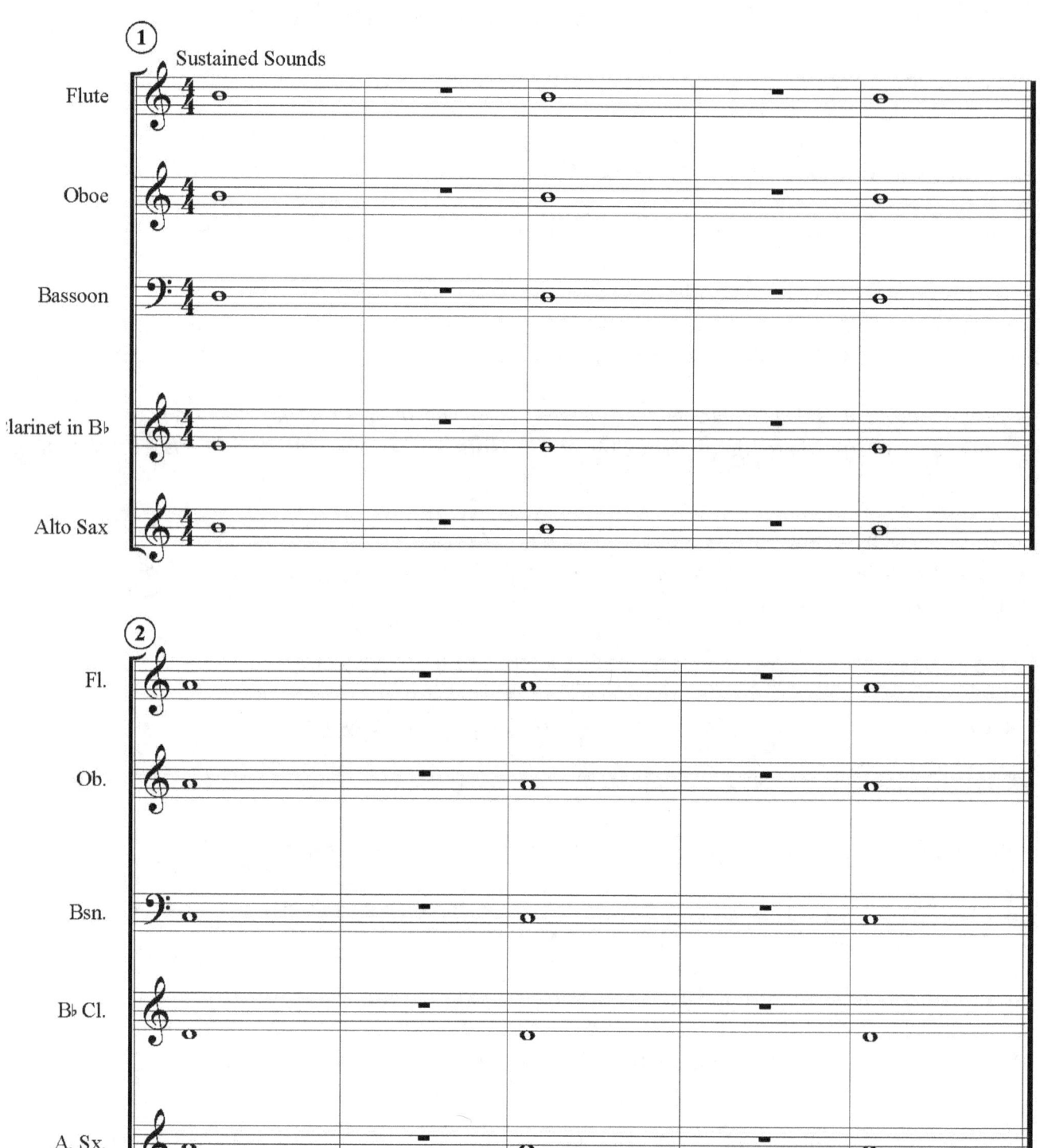

HETERGENEOUS WOODWIND EXERCISES

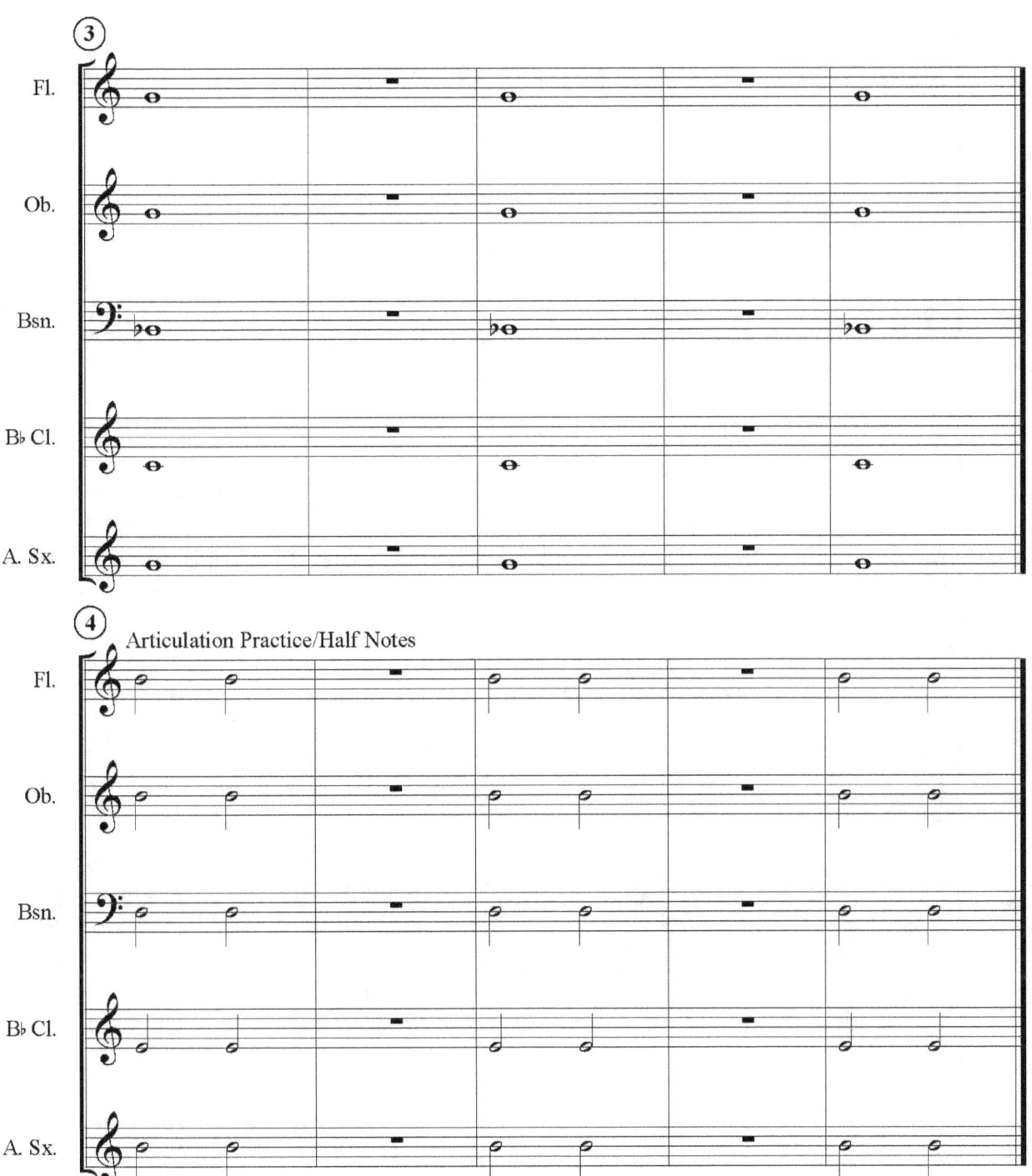

HETERGENEOUS WOODWIND EXERCISES

© 2025 Agogic Pres

Agogic Press grants permission to duplicate this worksheet for non-profit, educational use only, provided each copy includes this copyright notice.
Copies may not be sold or included in any materials offered for sale or for any form of profit.

HETERGENEOUS WOODWIND EXERCISES

© 2025 Agogic Press

Agogic Press grants permission to duplicate this worksheet for non-profit, educational use only, provided each copy includes this copyright notice. Copies may not be sold or included in any materials offered for sale or for any form of profit.

HETERGENEOUS WOODWIND EXERCISES

HETERGENEOUS WOODWIND EXERCISES

© 2025 Agogic Press

Agogic Press grants permission to duplicate this worksheet for non-profit, educational use only, provided each copy includes this copyright notice.
Copies may not be sold or included in any materials offered for sale or for any form of profit.

HETERGENEOUS WOODWIND EXERCISES

HETERGENEOUS WOODWIND EXERCISES

HETERGENEOUS WOODWIND EXERCISES

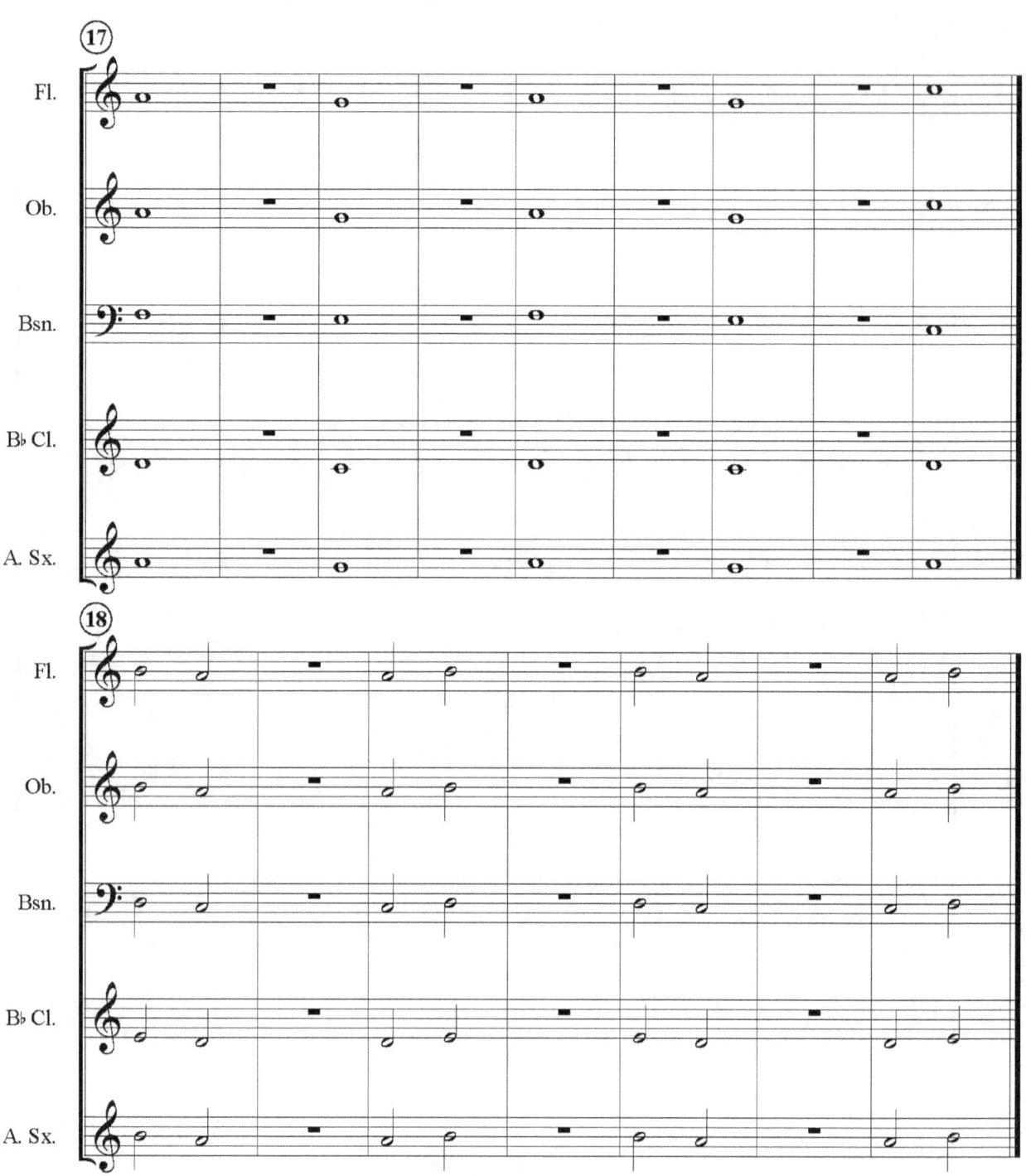

HETERGENEOUS WOODWIND EXERCISES

HETERGENEOUS WOODWIND EXERCISES

HETERGENEOUS WOODWIND EXERCISES

© 2025 Agogic Press

Agogic Press grants permission to duplicate this worksheet for non-profit, educational use only, provided each copy includes this copyright notice. Copies may not be sold or included in any materials offered for sale or for any form of profit.

HETERGENEOUS WOODWIND EXERCISES

HETERGENEOUS WOODWIND EXERCISES

HETERGENEOUS WOODWIND EXERCISES

HETERGENEOUS WOODWIND EXERCISES

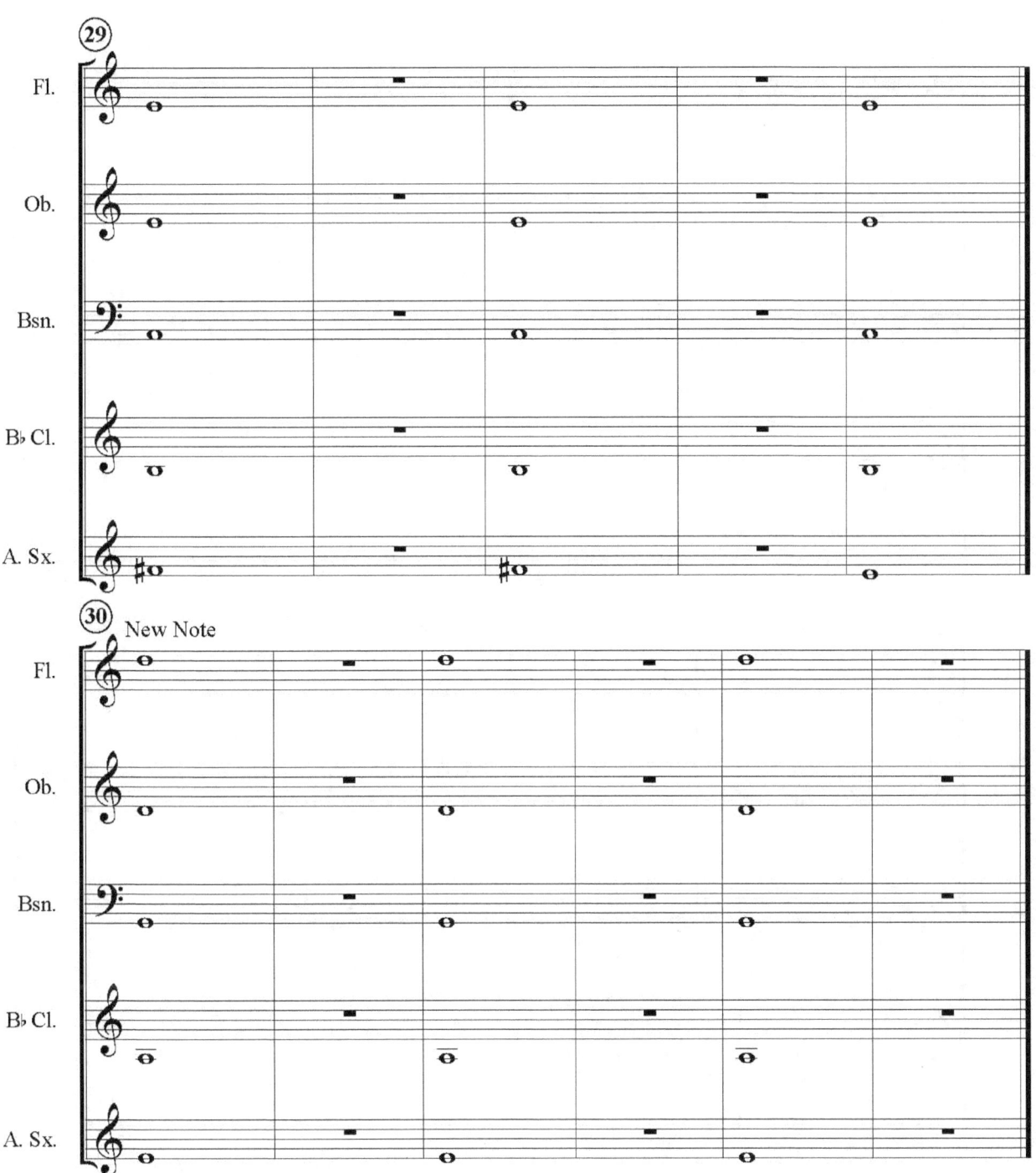

HETEROGENEOUS WOODWIND EXERCISES

HETERGENEOUS WOODWIND EXERCISES

HETERGENEOUS WOODWIND EXERCISES

HETERGENEOUS WOODWIND EXERCISES

HETERGENEOUS WOODWIND EXERCISES

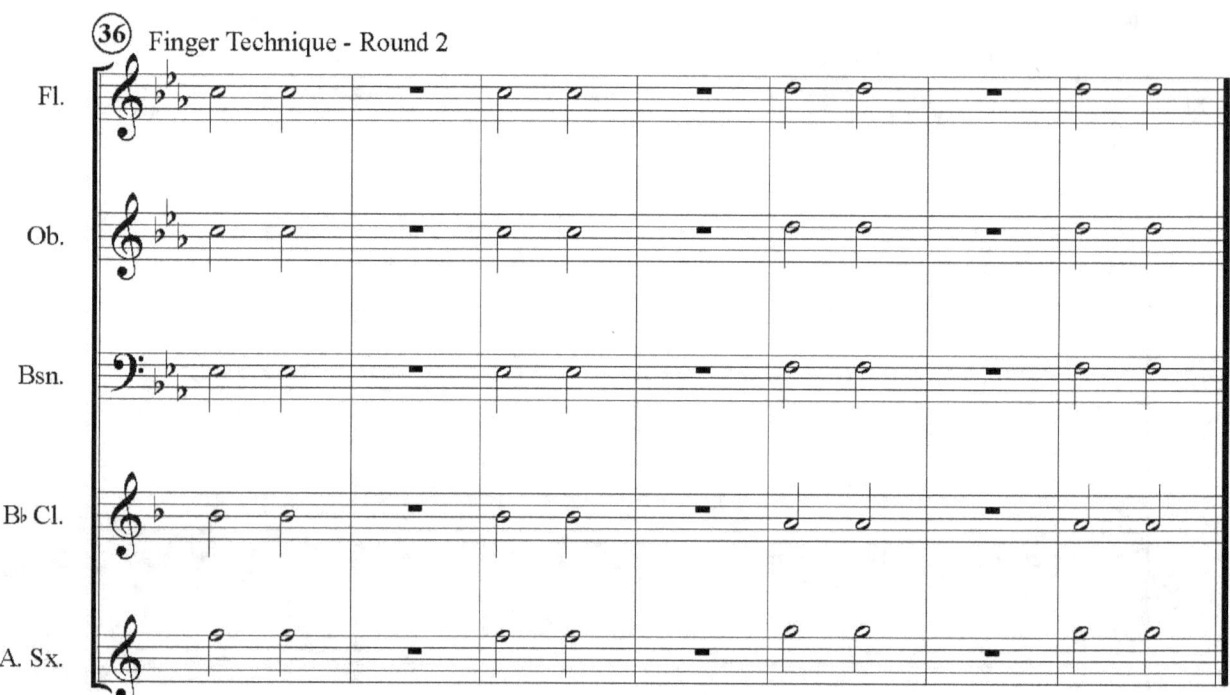

HETERGENEOUS WOODWIND EXERCISES

HETERGENEOUS WOODWIND EXERCISES

HETERGENEOUS WOODWIND EXERCISES

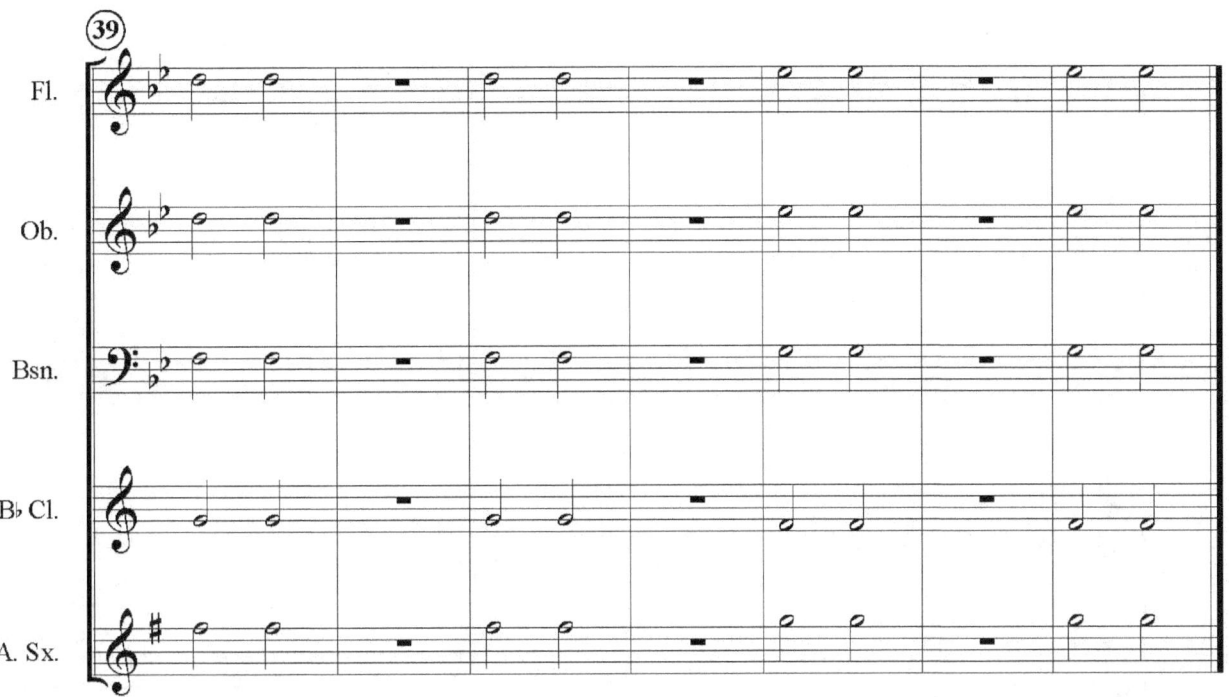

HETERGENEOUS WOODWIND EXERCISES

HETERGENEOUS WOODWIND EXERCISES

© 2025 Agogic Pres

Agogic Press grants permission to duplicate this worksheet for non-profit, educational use only, provided each copy includes this copyright notice.
Copies may not be sold or included in any materials offered for sale or for any form of profit.

HETERGENEOUS WOODWIND EXERCISES

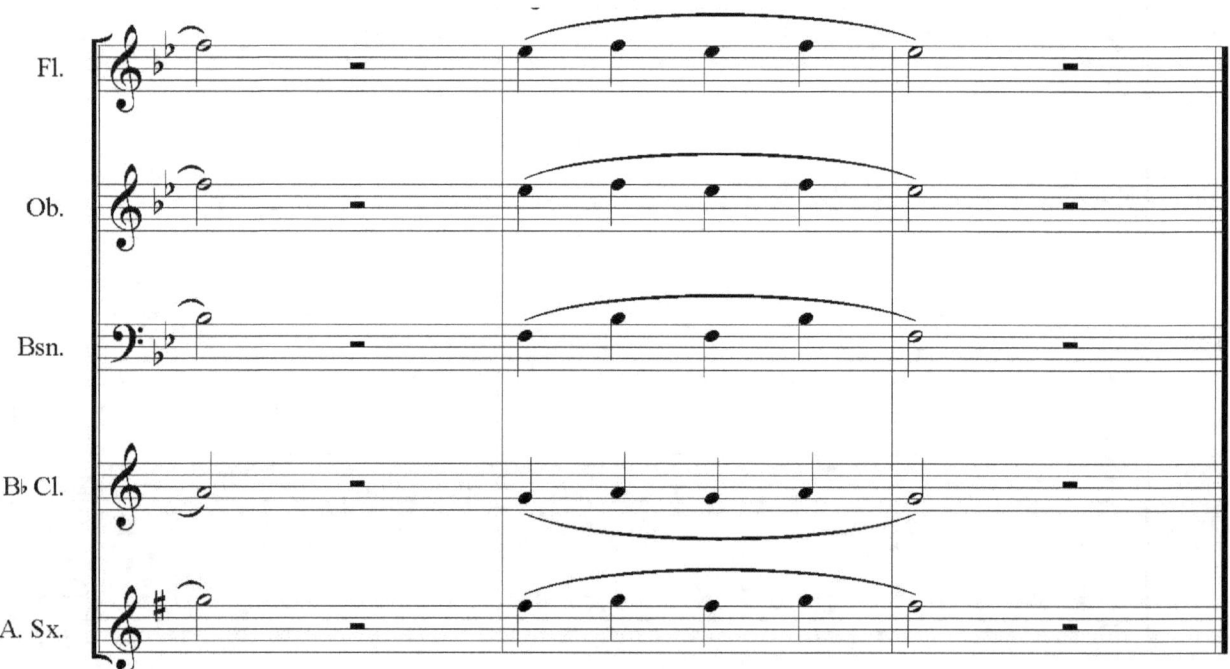

HETERGENEOUS WOODWIND EXERCISES

© 2025 Agogic Press

Agogic Press grants permission to duplicate this worksheet for non-profit, educational use only, provided each copy includes this copyright notice. Copies may not be sold or included in any materials offered for sale or for any form of profit.

HETERGENEOUS WOODWIND EXERCISES

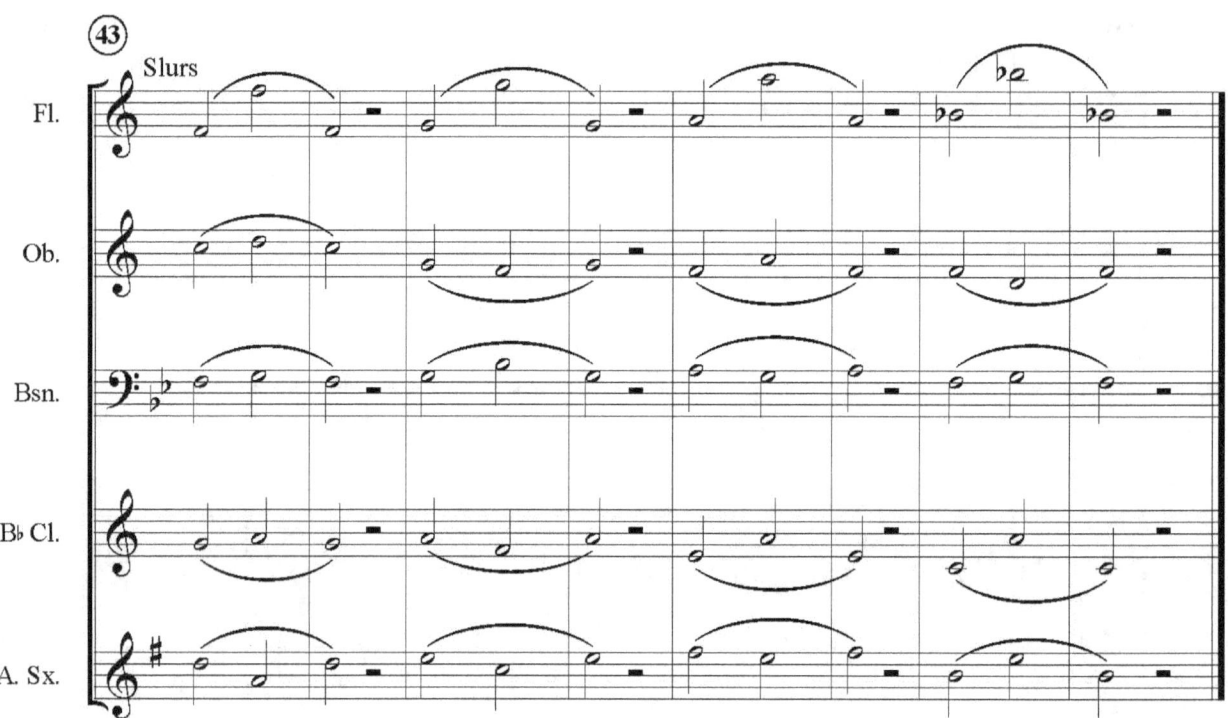

HETERGENEOUS WOODWIND EXERCISES

HETERGENEOUS WOODWIND EXERCISES

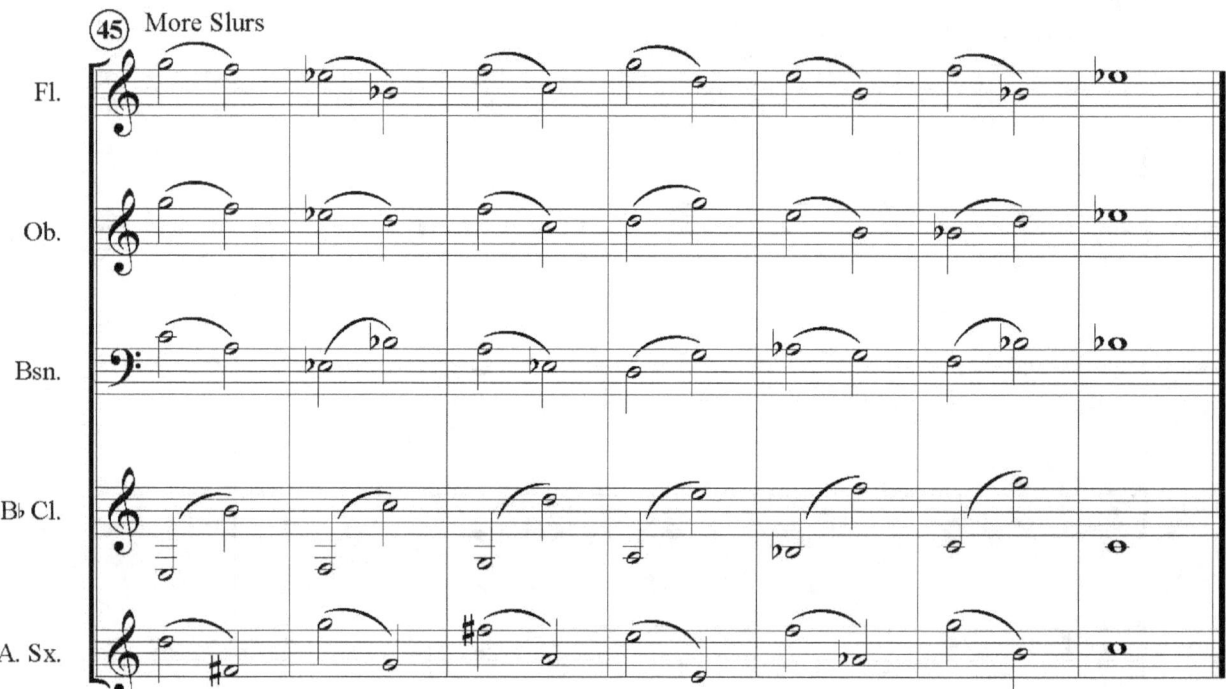

HETERGENEOUS WOODWIND EXERCISES

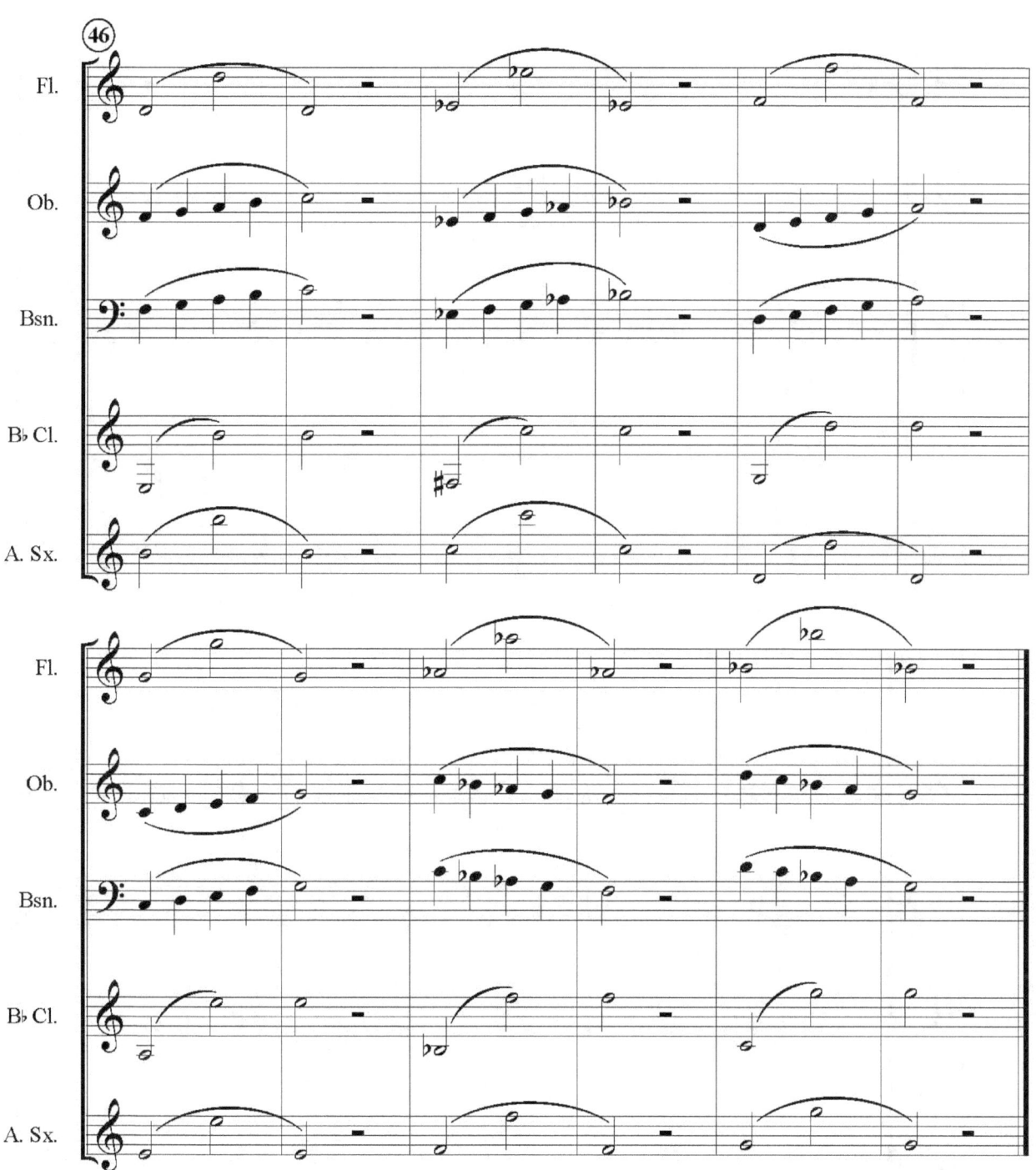

HETERGENEOUS WOODWIND EXERCISES

HETERGENEOUS WOODWIND EXERCISES

HETERGENEOUS WOODWIND EXERCISES

HETERGENEOUS WOODWIND EXERCISES

HETERGENEOUS WOODWIND EXERCISES

About the Author
JOHN DENIS

John Denis has sixteen years of experience working with Texas students at the public school and college levels. Dr. Denis creates and produces *Program Notes: The Band Director Podcast*, a program designed to help preservice and in-service directors find success in their own classrooms. He has been active as a clinician in Texas, and his writing has been featured in publications such as *Update: Applications of Research in Music Education; The Journal of Music, Technology, and Education; Contributions to Music Education;* and *The Southwestern Musician*.

He has also presented at the Texas Music Educators Association Clinic and Convention, the Midwest Clinic, the California All-State Music Education Conference, the Maryland Music Educators February Conference, the NAfME Music Research and Teacher Education National Conference, ISME World Conference, the International Research in Music Education Conference, the AERA Annual Meeting, and the NAfME Teacher In-service Conference. Along with Jordan Stern, Dr. Denis co-authored *Tuning with Technology: An Unofficial Guide to Tonal Energy and the Harmony Director*. He has had the opportunity to help several young band directors strengthen their teaching, which is definitely one of the perks of the job as far as he is concerned. He loves hearing from young band directors and helping in any way he can (so feel free to reach out).

Dr. Denis has a B.M. in music education from Texas Tech University as well as M.M.Ed. and Ph.D degrees from the University of North Texas and is currently on the music faculty at Texas State University in San Marcos, TX, where he teaches upper-level undergraduate and graduate music education courses, coordinates the music education program, completes music education scholarly work (like this book), and presents at conferences. He lives in the Austin area with his amazing wife Min Shien, where they love to explore the food scene and gather research for her food blog.

www.ingramcontent.com/pod-product-compliance
Lightning Source LLC
Chambersburg PA
CBHW080323080526

44585CB00021B/2450